Teachers Matter – But How?

Global processes are transforming educational policy around the world in complex ways, with different implications for different local arenas. Over the last two decades, a global neoliberal policy paradigm has emerged, placing the teacher at its centre. Two well-known examples are the OECD report on education and training policy, 'Teachers Matter', and the McKinsey & Company report entitled 'How the World's Best-Performing School Systems Come Out on Top'. It now seems more important than ever to highlight some alternatives that might contribute to a broader understanding of the meaning of being a teacher.

In a time of standardised performance and accountability, this special issue raises critical questions about the space for teachers' agency and teachers as curriculum agents. The different articles from some of our most distinguished researchers in the field provide essential perspectives on the question of where, when and how teachers matter. Our interest is not primarily to understand the scope of teachers' agency but rather to understand what becomes important for teachers in their everyday activities, such as teaching students, handling educational norms and rules, working in a local as well as a global society etc. A common theme throughout the articles is that teachers matter in spaces where they can act as moral subjects in their profession in the present, drawing on collective and individual experiences of the past whilst imagining a desired future.

The chapters in this book were originally published as a special issue of the *Journal of Curriculum Studies*.

Ninni Wahlström is Professor of Education at Linnæus University, Sweden. Her current research focuses on transnational and national policy discourses and their implications for national curriculum and classroom teaching from a perspective of critical curriculum theory. She is also interested in educational philosophy and theory, specifically in pragmatism. She is the author of *Transnational Curriculum Standards and Classroom Practices: The New Meaning of Teaching* (with Daniel Sundberg, 2017).

Daniel Alvunger is a Senior Lecturer in Education in the Department of Pedagogy and Learning at Linnæus University, Sweden. He is a member of the Studies in Curriculum, Teaching and Evaluation research group and his research concerns curriculum theory with a special focus on the complex and intertwined relations between transnational policy, national educational and curriculum reforms and the implications of reforms in local schools. His interests also include curriculum innovation, school development and educational leadership.

Daniel Sundberg is Professor of Education at Linnæus University, Sweden, where he is the co-leader of the Studies in Curriculum, Teaching and Evaluation research group. His main field of research is education reforms, curriculum and teaching, where changes over time and place in what counts as knowledge are central. More recently, he has investigated changing relations between educational research, politics of education and teaching practices from historical and comparative perspectives.

Teachers Matter – But How?

Edited by
Ninni Wahlström, Daniel Alvunger
and Daniel Sundberg

LONDON AND NEW YORK

First published 2018
by Routledge
2 Park Square, Milton Park, Abingdon, Oxon, OX14 4RN, UK

and by Routledge
711 Third Avenue, New York, NY 10017, USA

Routledge is an imprint of the Taylor & Francis Group, an informa business

Introduction, Chapters 1–2, 5–6 © 2018 Taylor and Francis
Chapter 3 © 2017 Gert Biesta, Mark Priestley and Sarah Robinson
Chapter 4 © 2017 Christine Winter

All rights reserved. No part of this book may be reprinted or reproduced or utilised in any form or by any electronic, mechanical, or other means, now known or hereafter invented, including photocopying and recording, or in any information storage or retrieval system, without permission in writing from the publishers.

Trademark notice: Product or corporate names may be trademarks or registered trademarks, and are used only for identification and explanation without intent to infringe.

British Library Cataloguing in Publication Data
A catalogue record for this book is available from the British Library

ISBN13: 978-1-138-54242-6

Typeset in MyriadPro
by diacriTech, Chennai

Publisher's Note
The publisher accepts responsibility for any inconsistencies that may have arisen during the conversion of this book from journal articles to book chapters, namely the possible inclusion of journal terminology.

Disclaimer
Every effort has been made to contact copyright holders for their permission to reprint material in this book. The publishers would be grateful to hear from any copyright holder who is not here acknowledged and will undertake to rectify any errors or omissions in future editions of this book.

Contents

Citation Information		vii
Notes on Contributors		ix
	Introduction: Teachers matter – but how?	1
	Daniel Alvunger, Daniel Sundberg and Ninni Wahlström	
1	Bearing witness to teaching and teachers	7
	David T. Hansen	
2	Global injustice, pedagogy and democratic iterations: some reflections on why teachers matter	24
	Elaine Unterhalter	
3	Talking about education: exploring the significance of teachers' talk for teacher agency	38
	Gert Biesta, Mark Priestley and Sarah Robinson	
4	Curriculum policy reform in an era of technical accountability: 'fixing' curriculum, teachers and students in English schools	55
	Christine Winter	
5	Accountability and control in American schools	75
	Richard M. Ingersoll and Gregory J. Collins	
6	Enacted realities in teachers' experiences: bringing materialism into pragmatism	96
	Elin Sundström Sjödin and Ninni Wahlström	
	Index	111

Citation Information

The chapters in this book were originally published in the *Journal of Curriculum Studies*, volume 49, issue 1 (February 2017). When citing this material, please use the original page numbering for each article, as follows:

Introduction
Teachers matter – but how?
Daniel Alvunger, Daniel Sundberg and Ninni Wahlström
Journal of Curriculum Studies, volume 49, issue 1 (February 2017) pp. 1–6

Chapter 1
Bearing witness to teaching and teachers
David T. Hansen
Journal of Curriculum Studies, volume 49, issue 1 (February 2017) pp. 7–23

Chapter 2
Global injustice, pedagogy and democratic iterations: some reflections on why teachers matter
Elaine Unterhalter
Journal of Curriculum Studies, volume 49, issue 1 (February 2017) pp. 24–37

Chapter 3
Talking about education: exploring the significance of teachers' talk for teacher agency
Gert Biesta, Mark Priestley and Sarah Robinson
Journal of Curriculum Studies, volume 49, issue 1 (February 2017) pp. 38–54

Chapter 4
Curriculum policy reform in an era of technical accountability: 'fixing' curriculum, teachers and students in English schools
Christine Winter
Journal of Curriculum Studies, volume 49, issue 1 (February 2017) pp. 55–74

Chapter 5
Accountability and control in American schools
Richard M. Ingersoll and Gregory J. Collins
Journal of Curriculum Studies, volume 49, issue 1 (February 2017) pp. 75–95

CITATION INFORMATION

Chapter 6

Enacted realities in teachers' experiences: bringing materialism into pragmatism
Elin Sundström Sjödin and Ninni Wahlström
Journal of Curriculum Studies, volume 49, issue 1 (February 2017) pp. 96–110

For any permission-related enquiries please visit:
http://www.tandfonline.com/page/help/permissions

Notes on Contributors

Daniel Alvunger is a Senior Lecturer in Education in the Department of Pedagogy and Learning at Linnæus University, Sweden. He is a member of the Studies in Curriculum, Teaching and Evaluation research group and his research concerns curriculum theory with a special focus on the complex and intertwined relations between transnational policy, national educational and curriculum reforms and the implications of reforms in local schools. His interests also include curriculum innovation, school development and educational leadership.

Gert Biesta is Professor of Education and Director of Research in the Department of Education of Brunel University, London, UK. His work focuses on the theory and philosophy of education and the theory and philosophy of educational and social research, with a particular interest in questions of democracy and democratization. His books include *The Beautiful Risk of Education* (2004) and *Art, Artists and Pedagogy: Philosophy and the Arts in Education* (with Naughton and Cole, 2017).

Gregory J. Collins is currently studying towards a PhD in Education Policy at the University of Pennsylvania, Philadelphia, PA, USA. His research interests centre on teacher and educational leadership policy. He has previously worked as a high school teacher.

David T. Hansen is a Professor in the Historical and Philosophical Foundations of Education, and the Director of the Program in Philosophy and Education, at Teachers College, Columbia University, New York, NY, USA. He has written widely on teaching, including in books such as *The Call to Teach* (1995), *Exploring the Moral Heart of Teaching* (2001), *Ethical Visions of Education* (2007) and *The Teacher and the World* (2011). He is a past-president of both the Philosophy of Education Society and the John Dewey Society, and is a fellow of the American Educational Research Association.

Richard M. Ingersoll is Professor of Education and Sociology, and Board of Overseers Chair of Education, at the University of Pennsylvania, Philadelphia, PA, USA. His research is concerned with the character of elementary and secondary schools as workplaces, teachers as employees and teaching as a job.

Mark Priestley is Professor of Education and Director of the Stirling Network for Curriculum Studies at the University of Stirling, UK. His research interests relate to the school curriculum and the professional work of teachers, and his recent work has focused on Scotland's Curriculum for Excellence, with critical analysis of the CfE model and empirical research around teachers' work as they develop the curriculum. He is the editor of *Reinventing the Curriculum: New Trends in Curriculum Policy and Practice* (with

NOTES ON CONTRIBUTORS

Gert Biesta, 2013) and author of *Teacher Agency: An Ecological Approach* (with Gert Biesta and Sarah Robinson, 2015).

Sarah Robinson is Associate Professor at the Centre for Teaching Development and Digital Media at Aarhus University, Denmark. She is an educational anthropologist whose research interests span from policy in practice, curriculum reform and education bureaucracy to teacher agency. Her current research focuses on enterprise education as a method in the Humanities and Arts in Higher Education.

Daniel Sundberg is Professor of Education at Linnæus University, Sweden, where he is the co-leader of the Studies in Curriculum, Teaching and Evaluation research group. His main field of research is education reforms, curriculum and teaching, where changes over time and place in what counts as knowledge are central. More recently, he has investigated changing relations between educational research, politics of education and teaching practices from historical and comparative perspectives.

Elin Sundström Sjödin is a PhD student in the Department of Humanities, Education and Social Sciences at Örebro University, Sweden. The research for her dissertation focuses on the reading of literature in schools. She draws on pragmatic and socio-material theories in order to investigate how reading and literature is enacted and valuated in educational settings.

Elaine Unterhalter is Professor of Education and International Development at the University College London Institute of Education, UK. She has written extensively on global inequalities, education and the capability approach. Her current research concerns education, poverty and global social justice. She is the author of *Education, Poverty and Global Goals for Gender Equality* (with Amy North, 2017).

Ninni Wahlström is Professor of Education at Linnæus University, Sweden. Her current research focuses on transnational and national policy discourses and their implications for national curriculum and classroom teaching from a perspective of critical curriculum theory. She is also interested in educational philosophy and theory, specifically in pragmatism. She is the author of *Transnational Curriculum Standards and Classroom Practices: The New Meaning of Teaching* (with Daniel Sundberg, 2017).

Christine Winter is Senior Lecturer in Educational Studies at the University of Sheffield, UK, and Education Pathway Lead for the White Rose Doctoral Training Centre, a postgraduate training consortium of the Universities of Sheffield, Leeds and York. Her research focuses on the secondary school curriculum with specific interests in curriculum knowledge, politics, policy and practice, globalization and global citizenship education.

INTRODUCTION

Teachers matter – but how?

Daniel Alvunger, Daniel Sundberg and Ninni Wahlström

'School is a place where tests are failed and passed, where amusing things happen, where new insights are stumbled upon, and skills acquired' (Jackson, 1990). We all know what a school is and we all know that our assumptions of what a school is differ depending who it is who knows. Our knowing about school matters, because it is largely from our understanding of the school's task we shape our notion of a 'good' teacher and the characteristics of valuable and important teaching.

In this special issue, we start from a general policy assumption about teachers and teaching particularly clearly summarized in the 2005 report *Teachers Matter: Attracting, Developing and Retaining Effective Teachers* by the Organisation for Economic Co-Operation and Development (OECD). The report states that teacher policy is high on national agendas and that teachers are 'the most significant resource in schools' for improving efficiency and equity in school. Thus, the policy report states school improvement largely depends on 'ensuring that competent people want to work as teachers, that their teaching is of high quality, and that all students have access to high quality teaching' (OECD, 2005, p. 7). Against a background of an increasingly centralized transnational and national governance of school, emphasizing international comparisons (Dale & Robertson, 2009; Lawn & Grek, 2012; Meyer & Benavot, 2013; Nordin & Sundberg, 2014; Rizvi & Lingard, 2010) and a curriculum characterized by performativity and educational effectiveness (Ball, 2003; Kelly, 2009), we are interested in teachers' significance and conditions for teacher agency. However, we regard the policy field mainly as the background, from which we retain the fundamental claim that 'teachers matter'. In contrast to policy documents, the intention in this special issue is to explore in what different ways, at what different times and in what different spaces teachers truly matter, without having any answers in advance – that is, outside the area of policy highroads but still against a backdrop of a policy of accountability and standards.

A temporal understanding of curriculum and teacher agency

Conceptions of school and teaching influence the way teachers think about teaching and how they actually conduct their work in the classroom. With reference to Hansen (2001), teaching has its own integrity. Teaching here is viewed as a moral and intellectual practice developed from within the person, rather than getting one's norms imposed from outside. Through our subjectivity, we can begin to know ourselves and the world we inhabit, imprinted by culture and history. Genuine learning and growth, for teachers and their students, cannot be hastened; it is a process with its own dimension of time. Teachers' professional identities, who they are and the meanings teachers attribute to their work and the meanings that are attributed to them by others, are shaped not only by organizational and subject-related aspects but also by their relationships to colleagues, students and parents and a life outside of school (Day & Gu, 2010).

We suggest that it is helpful to understand curriculum in its verb form when we want to include several aspects of curriculum, for example the official curriculum, the implicit curriculum and the 'null curriculum', that is, what is omitted from curriculum (Eisner, 1979). The verb form of curriculum suggested by Pinar, Reynolds, Slattery, and Taubman (2004) is *currere*, emphasizing the lived experience of curriculum. Cherryholmes (2002) parallels the reciprocal dependence of curriculum/*currere* with the curriculum/non-curriculum distinction noted by Eisner (1979). In order to conceptualize the complex field that represents teachers' action arena, we need to understand the teacher's role as the one who transforms curriculum into practical teaching, with all the actual choices of inclusions and exclusions that such a transformation requires, and the one who converts the curriculum content into a form that becomes intelligibly and interesting for pupils. In this process, teachers can handle curriculum texts 'as artists' who choose within the limits of the situations in which they find themselves, 'how to conceptualize curriculum/*currere*' (Cherryholmes, 2002, p. 125), that is how to make a distinction between the course of study and the way it will be experienced. By understanding teaching as a curriculum event, Doyle (1992) uses the verb to 'author' curriculum. Teaching is understood as a curriculum process, which means that classrooms are contexts in which students encounter curriculum events when teachers link the institutional curriculum to the classroom context. These curriculum events in classroom settings become jointly constructed by teachers and students in their authoring and responding roles.

Schools and schooling have consequences by virtue of what they teach and what they avoid teaching. Teachers and students are individual subjects who experience curricula in a combination of content and the way it is taught, as well as the way some content is left outside. In addition, the administrative systems which manifest in terms of accountability and different forms of control systems need to be included in the three forms of curriculum mentioned above. Through an understanding of curriculum and being a teacher as activities taking place in certain environments structured by time and space, it becomes possible to perceive teacher agency as reconstructions: as a re-assembling of the past, a re-anticipation of the future and a re-understanding of the presence. Subjectivity and subjective reconstructions '[require] installing sharp distinctions among the three temporal domains in order to forestall their blurring and to enable memory, morality, and agency' (Pinar, 2011, p. 159). To learn anything from the presence, individually and collectively, we need to remember the past as well as foresee some of the future. In a study of teacher agency, Emirbayer and Mische (1998) have emphasized the importance of comprehending agency as temporality also in an analytical sense. They therefore define agency as a temporally constructed engagement, based on the habits, imagination and judgements of what seems best to do at the present with respect to what has been and what one wants to achieve.

Where, when and how teachers matter

Teacher agency can be defined in moral terms of what it means to be a teacher in terms of professionalism and what it means to be a person in terms of subjectivity. Phrased in this way, teaching is viewed as a moral activity enacted in an environment where humans and non-human things of importance interact. Environment here is understood in Dewey's (1916/2008) notion of the word as attention to these things to which a person relate, modify, change, adapt, etc. Actors in different structural environments reproduce and change those structures through their interaction with people and things of concern, based on remembrance of the history, hope for the future and a desire to do the best of the present. With Latour's (2005, p. 217) words, an actor could not act without the large network of attachments of mediators transforming and translating the meaning of the elements it mediates, by *making* other mediators *do* things'. Policy, curriculum, national tests and so on are certainly some of the mediators, but not the only ones. As we can see from the articles in this special issue, the students are the ones who are most often are at the centre of teacher agency, making teachers 'do things' in certain ways.

In this special issue, based on a research conference held at Linnæus University in Sweden 2014, we explore a common theme titled *Teachers Matter – But How?* In a time of standardized performance and accountability, this special issue raises critical questions about the space for teachers' epistemic agency and teachers as curriculum agents. The different articles provide essential perspectives on the question of where, when and how teachers matter. Our interest is not primarily to understand the scope of teachers' agency but rather to understand what becomes important for teachers in their everyday activities, as teaching students, handling educational norms and rules, working in a local as well as a global society, etc. By understanding the primacy of temporality in curriculum (Cherryholmes, 2002; Pinar, 2011) and teacher agency (Emirbayer & Mische, 1998), we conceptualize teachers' significance as formed by 'the moment of vision' (Huebner, 1967, p. 178). With reference to Huebner's elements of the education environment, teacher matters when they envision a potentiality in the past–present–future dimension that is uniquely human and 'requires the presence of human wisdom' (p. 179). Thus, teachers matter in spaces where they can act as moral subjects in their profession in the present, drawing on collective and individual experiences of the past whilst imagining a desired future.

In the first article 'Bearing witness to teaching and teachers', David Hansen poses the philosophical question what it means to be a person in the world today. More specifically, he wonders what it means to be a person in the role of teacher today. He strives to grasp those broad questions through the concept of 'bearing witness'. Based on a field study, Hansen introduces the orientation of bearing witness to teaching and teachers through the field notes from the teacher Karolina's classroom. To capture the contours and consequences for educational work, intellectual, aesthetic and moral aspects of teaching as well as of education research are combined in this orientation of research. To witness means to be in the same place as someone else and trying to understand also what happens behind what appears to happen. There is nothing predetermined in bearing witness; instead, the intention is to cultivate an ethical and dynamic relation to the everyday world of the school and the role of the teacher for understanding what it means to be a teacher in the world. The individual is at centre of the study, and the interest is focused on what relations and experiences that are shaping her subjectivity as a person and as a teacher. Through elucidating the importance of remembrance, wisdom and possible potential, this form of research can remind policy actors as well as the public of the efforts needed for genuine human encounters to come into being. In his study, Hansen demonstrates how the students and their teacher are involved in forming themselves as subjects.

In the article 'Global injustice, pedagogy and democratic iterations: Some reflections on why teachers matter', Elaine Unterhalter understands pedagogic relationships as a form of democratic iteration. Drawing on the concept of democratic iteration, formulated by Seyla Benhabib, Unterhalter explores what it means to involve teachers and students in processes of critical reflections on inequalities that emerge in the local classroom, however, embedded in a globally connected world. By developing the concept of a pedagogical relationship linked with democratic iterations, Unterhalter formulates the relation between education and equity in terms of 'inequality of what', 'inequality of whom' and 'inequality of how'. From her experiences as a university teacher, Unterhalter theoretically problematizes a striving to handle the injustices and inequalities of our contemporary world. She demonstrates the fragility of pedagogical relationships and the difficulties in trying to listen to silenced and oppressed voices in today's global classrooms. Teachers matter because teachers' responses, situated in certain structures of time and space, have consequences for the students, also in relation to occurrences that are historically and geographically distant. For the students we meet in this study, the presence is permeated by the past, explicitly or in silence, and by hope or fear for the future. The pedagogical relationship concerns equity from the bottom, from the middle and from above in society, relating to different forms of cosmopolitanism.

In the third article 'Talking about education: Exploring the significance of teachers' talk for teacher agency', by Gert Biesta, Mark Priestley and Sarah Robinson, teacher agency is explored and analysed. In order to map out the research field of teacher knowledge, the article starts with the distinctions from Shulman on teachers' professional knowledge. The research interest in the article is directed towards teachers' personal practical knowledge (with reference to Joseph Schwab) as complementary to teachers' propositional knowledge. Of special concern is the narrative dimension of experiential and personal encounters with practical issues. This understanding of teacher knowledge and teacher agency is grounded in an ecological approach that also takes into account the structures and cultures of teachers' professional life and practices. The achievement of agency is thus seen as a capacity that is framed by structural and contextual ecological conditions. Biesta, Priestley and Robinson argue for overcoming an one-sidedness of teacher agency approaches and stress a dynamic interplay of three interrelated dimensions of iterational, projective and practical evaluative aspects of teachers' work (drawing on Emirbayer & Mische, 1998). In the empirical analyses of seven semi-structured teacher interviews, the dimensions of teachers' agency via bio-graphical narratives are explored. The cases present nuanced, aspect-rich and deepened illustrations of the dynamic interplay of structural, contextual and biographical conditions at play in achieving agency.

The article by Christine Winter, 'Curriculum policy reform in an era of technical account-ability: "Fixing" curriculum, teachers and students in English schools', highlights a recent curriculum reform in England with special attention to how teachers in 'disadvantaged' sec-ondary schools make sense of and experience the changes concerning the subjects History and Geography within a programme of study undertaken by students aged 13–16 years in England (the General Certificate of Secondary Education [GSCE]). In this small-scale study in terms of a pilot study, the word 'fix' – from its various meanings – is used as an overarching word and for trying to capture salient features and intentions of policy-makers with the new curriculum, e.g. claims to 'fix' the education system or 'the teachers'. At the heart of the analysis are the concepts of 'technical accountability' and 'ethical responsibility'. Winter describes technical accountability through the impact of standardized testing, the selection and narrowing of content in core subjects and the emphasis on literacy and numeracy as primary capabilities. Added to this is the trend of transforming students into 'data' as a consequence of increased demands for standardization, measurement and computerization. Winter argues that the dominating technical–rational discourse of educational policy-making neglects 'the ethical importance of the singularity and uniqueness of the subject and of human relationality in education'. One of the implications of the recent curriculum reform according to Winter thus is a kind of 'de-humanisation' in which the teacher's professionalism and autonomy are eroded and where the room for action, spontaneity and creativity is reduced in order to be aligned with curriculum and assessment criteria.

The theme of standardization and accountability is also addressed in the article by Richard Ingersoll and Gregory Collins, 'Accountability and control in American schools'. The authors examine the question of accountability and teacher quality. This issue has been highly debated and even controversial not only in the USA, which is the case in the article, but also internationally. Ingersoll and Collins provide a needed theoretical analysis and empirical validation. The article argues for the need to take the specific character of the teaching occupation and its organization into account when diagnosing the issues. The predominant teacher-deficit viewpoint is thus put in a critical light. Instead of merely focusing on deficits in the chain of delivery, the argument that is unfolded in the article is that a sound diagnosis should include a widened and contextualized approach to the issue of accountability and teacher quality. The article identifies blind spots in contemporary educational and curriculum research as well as policy discourses. Various reforms since the No Child Left Behind Act (NCLB) in 2002 have operated by these assumptions, the article argues. Ingersoll and Collins claim that although the theory of accountability is widely accepted, and rightly point at some important issues and problems, it is nevertheless problematic. It needs to be complemented with a sound sociology of organizations and occupations and the specific character of teachers' work. The article makes a case for overcoming a kind of prominent one-sidedness in thinking about teacher accountability. A balanced approach to teacher accountability, which is argued for, acknowledges the need for teacher accountability, but rather than top-down accountability reforms, it includes giving power and control of key school and classroom decisions to schools and teachers.

The sixth and final article, 'Enacted realities in teachers' experiences: Bringing materialism into pragmatism' by Elin Sundström Sjödin and Ninni Wahlström, addresses a recent discussion within curriculum theory research concerning the revived interest in realism. More specifically, Sundström-Sjödin and Wahlström seek to theoretically develop connections between Dewey's 'transactional realism' and actor–network theory (ANT) within new materialism. The purpose is to contribute to a deepened understanding of factors and phenomena that shape the conditions for and influence the work of teachers, regardless of being outside of or inside of the school as institution. ANT is used to identify networks and actors that are of importance for teachers' actions. Drawing from the work of Latour of 'mediators' that translate and transform meanings, Sundström-Sjödin and Wahlström argue that actors may be affected by human as well as non-human mediators. Empirically, the article explores grading as a teacher practice through the example of the teacher Susan. From Susan's description of parental pressure in her work with grading, it becomes clear how she is influenced by the principal, the demands from parents and pupils and the digital communication system with its email technology. Following Sundström-Sjödin and Wahlström's argument, the email system functions as a mediator. The question that can be asked is not necessarily how the teacher makes judgments when he or she grades, but rather 'where is grading?' By identifying socio-material processes including human and material factors, the article adds a new and widening perspective on in what complex ways teachers' actions are shaped and how the border between the private and professional becomes blurred.

References

Ball, S. J. (2003). The teacher's soul and the terrors of performativity. *Journal of Education Policy, 18*, 215–228.

Cherryholmes, C. H. (2002). Curriculum ghosts and visions – and what to do? In W. E. Doll & N. Gough (Eds.), *Curriculum visions* (pp. 116–126). New York, NY: Peter Lang.

Dale, R., & Robertson, S. (Eds.). (2009). *Globalisation & Europeanisation in education*. Oxford: Symposium Books.

Day, C., & Gu, Q. (2010). *The new lives of teachers*. Oxon: Routledge.

Dewey, J. (1916/2008). Democracy and education. In J. A. Boydston (Ed.), *John Dewey. The middle works, 1899–1924. Vol. 9: 1916* (pp. 3–370). Carbondale: Southern Illinois University Press.

Doyle, W. (1992). Curriculum and pedagogy. In P. W. Jackson (Ed.), *Handbook of research on curriculum* (pp. 486–516). New York, NY: Macmillan.

Eisner, E. W. (1979). *The educational imagination: On the design and evaluation of school programs*. New York, NY: Macmillan.

Emirbayer, M., & Mische, A. (1998). What is agency? *American Journal of Sociology, 103*, 962–1023.

Hansen, D. T. (2001). *Exploring the moral heart of teaching*. New York, NY: Teachers College Press.

Huebner, D. (1967). Curriculum as concern for man's temporality. *Theory Into Practice, 6*, 172–179.

Jackson, P. W. (1990). *Life in classrooms*. New York, NY: Teachers College Press.

Kelly, A. V. (2009). *The curriculum: Theory and practice*. London: Sage.

Latour, B. (2005). *Reassembling the social: An introduction to actor-network-theory*. Oxford: Oxford University Press.

Lawn, M., & Grek, S. (2012). *Europeanizing education: Governing a new policy space*. Oxford: Symposium Books.

Meyer, H. D., & Benavot, A. (2013). *PISA, power, and policy: The emergence of global educational governance. Oxford studies in comparative education*. Oxford: Symposium Books.

Nordin, A., & Sundberg, D. (Eds.). (2014). *Transnational policy flows in European education: The making and governing of knowledge in the education policy field. Oxford studies in comparative education*. Oxford: Symposium Books.

Organisation for Economic Co-operation and Development. (2005). *Teachers matter: Attracting, developing and retaining effective teachers*. Paris: Author.

Pinar, W. F. (2011). *The character of curriculum studies*. New York, NY: Palgrave Macmillan.

Pinar, W. F., Reynolds, W. M., Slattery, P., & Taubman, P. M. (2004). *Understanding curriculum: An introduction to the study of historical and contemporary curriculum discourses*. New York, NY: Peter Lang.

Rizvi, F., & Lingard, B. (2010). *Globalizing education policy*. London: Routledge.

Bearing witness to teaching and teachers

David T. Hansen

ABSTRACT

In this article, the author elucidates the idea of bearing witness to teaching and teachers. The orientation derives from a philosophical and field-based inquiry pivoting around the questions What does it mean to be a person in the world today? and What does it mean to be a person in the role of teacher? From 2012 to 2014, the author interacted closely with 16 teachers from 8 different state-funded schools in a large, culturally diverse US city. The endeavor included extensive classroom visits, whole-group discussion meetings, and a systematic series of individual interviews. The article shows how the orientation of bearing witness calls fresh attention to the person who occupies the role of teacher. It illuminates the easy-to-overlook truth that it is persons, rather than roles as such, who educate. The author argues that bearing witness contributes importantly to remembrance of deep educational values.

The path of things is silent. Will they suffer a speaker to go with them?

Ralph Waldo Emerson, 'The Poet' (1983, p. 459)

1. Introduction

'Bearing witness' is a familiar term. There is the witness in court who attests to the facts of a case. There is the witness at a wedding, a bank, or a law office, who signs a formal document and attests, thereby, to the validity of what has transpired. The religious witness expresses a revelation or an insight into scripture. The social witness rejects a hierarchical social order and elects to live amongst the poor, the downtrodden, and the marginalized. Many persons have sought to bear witness to large-scale human trauma, such as the atrocities of World War II. Here, the witness calls for a moral awakening, for justice, for remembrance, even while meticulously recording the facts of violence (Agamben, 2002; Felman & Laub, 1992; Hatley, 2000; Oliver, 2001; Simon, 2005). Significantly, in all these uses of the concept, the witness is not 'complete' until it has been shared and acknowledged by others. Witnessing comes to life in communication (Peters, 2001).

TEACHERS MATTER – BUT HOW?

Scholars have begun to draw out the educational ramifications of forms of witnessing associated with historical trauma. Their work foregrounds a normative rather than merely descriptive framing of the concept (see e.g. Berlak, 1999; Di Paolantonio, 2015; Hansen, 2012; Ropers-Huilman, 1999; Zembylas, 2006) The idea of bearing witness to teaching and teachers that I elucidate here takes its point of departure from a different though morally allied origin, especially with respect to fundamental questions of human dignity and recognition. The context for the study is a recently completed philosophical and field-based inquiry involving myself, two doctoral research assistants, and 16 teachers from 8 different state-funded schools in the same culturally diverse metropolitan setting. The animating questions for the inquiry were: What does it mean to be a person in the world today? and What does it mean to be a person in the role of teacher today? For two years, my assistants and I sat in on several hundred classes taught by the teachers. I myself devoted 74 days to classroom visits, typically spending 2–3 h on each occasion bearing witness to a teacher's world. We met with the teachers as a group 21 times for wide-ranging discussion of the project themes. Each meeting included a modest catered dinner and lasted 3 h. We also recorded and transcribed 42 individual interviews with the participants.[1]

The questions about being a person were born from a fusion of philosophical wonder and practical concern. Much of my career has involved working with teachers. I remain endlessly struck by a wondrous, dynamic fact that goes unremarked because it is so familiar: namely, that there are human beings who render themselves into what we call 'teachers', and who have a genuinely positive influence on other human beings. Behind this source of wonder is the timeless question of who or what we are as beings, encompassing in turn the questions of why we are here at all (the profound mystery of why is there something rather than nothing) and how we should conduct our lives in light of the primordial fact, or gift, of our 'isness'.

Alongside reverberating wonder, the concern motivating the two-year-long study emerged from an increasingly unsettled sense that the integrity of teaching as a practice, indeed as a calling to many of its practitioners, is in danger of being sundered (at least in the US) by today's so-called 'accountability' policies. These policies are premised upon cost-benefit and bottom-line business mentalities that are constitutionally unable to approach teaching as the complex intellectual, moral, and social endeavor it has always been. Good teaching requires a continuously developing sense of judgment regarding how to engage students in subject matter, how to interpret their understanding, how to draw upon their experience to help them perceive the significance of their studies, how to cultivate a supportive learning community in the classroom, and much more (Hostetler, 1997, 2011; Sherman, 2013; Sockett, 2012). But instead of creating mechanisms to enrich the development of good judgment in the classroom, current policy marginalizes or undermines it (Santoro, 2011a, 2011b, 2013; Wills & Sandholtz, 2009). The moral baseline in the present article is the view that teachers are *singular persons* who, with the right support, bring commitment, knowledge, a sympathetic outlook, and other human offerings to their work with the young.

Bearing witness has a family resemblance with several well-known modes of research: phenomenology, portraiture, connoisseurship (with its close relation, educational criticism), and arts-based inquiry. The orientation resembles phenomenology in its attention to fundamental signs and indices of what is sometimes summarized as 'being-in-the-world,' in this case the teacher's. Phenomenological method involves scrupulous, detailed description of human action, undertaken not with an a priori hypothesis or with a desire to explain on a cause-effect basis, but rather with the aim of helping others perceive the easy-to-overlook concreteness and complexity of lived experience (Van Manen, 1990, 2014).

Witnessing resembles portraiture in that both aspire to present an educator's world in a spirit of critical sympathy, with an equal accent on both of those terms (Dewey, 1985, pp. 127, 128, 155, 1989, p. 270). Portraiture seeks to capture educators' efforts 'to do the right thing' from a professional point of view (Lawrence-Lightfoot, 2005; Lawrence-Lightfoot & Hoffman Davis, 1997). Portraiture and phenomenology, as I understand them, entail neither approval nor disapproval of teachers and teaching. They differ from social engineering research that presumes a deficit model of teachers, and they differ from what become, in effect, hagiographies. Phenomenology and portraiture illuminate the poetics of teaching (Hansen, 2004; Stillwaggon, 2016): how a teacher's aesthetic, moral, and intellectual sensibility finds expression through the most (seemingly) ordinary things she or he enacts in the classroom.

The orientation to teaching I call bearing witness also evokes what Elliot Eisner dubs connoisseurship with its attendant capacity for fine-grained criticism (Eisner, 1976, 1991). Connoisseurship, at first glance, may conjure an elitist image of a moneyed collector of paintings or fine wines. However, Eisner democratizes the concept in showing how it points to a human potentiality that can apply equally to one of the arts, to plumbing, to building roads, to piloting an aircraft—and to undertaking educational research. Connoisseurship denotes how a person can develop, through extensive experience and reflection, a rich, nuanced feeling for and understanding of a particular activity. This immersion positions the person, in turn, to become an insightful critic of that activity: thus Eisner's emphasis on what he calls educational criticism, mirroring the deeply grounded perspective of the literary or art critic. The inquirer-as-witness to teaching must bring to bear an experiential as well as scholarly intimacy with the dynamics of the practice.

Finally, bearing witness resembles arts-based research (Barone & Eisner, 2012). It does so, in part, by taking the artist as an exemplar of disciplined inquiry. Successful artists are no more interested in 'subjective impressions' and 'anecdotal evidence' than are successful scientists. Rather, their extraordinary focus, their persistent self-questioning, their commitment to truth, their command of technique, their sheer hard work, and more, constitute a warrant for trusting them that is every bit as significant as what scientists construct through their methods. Science attempts to explain. Art illuminates meaning. Human beings live in and by meaning, including the meaning they ascribe to explanations. Arts-based inquiry attends to the meaning people variously find, lose, create, discover, and yearn for in their lives.

The modes of research touched on above have yielded valuable insights about educational practice. They have widened the circle of what counts as research, demonstrating why the social sciences have their value but not a monopoly on how to grasp educational reality. These modes echo John Dewey's wise remark: 'Truth telling is a duty for all, but it is not the duty of all to tell the same truth, because they have not the same truth to tell' (1971, pp. 317, 318). The orientation of bearing witness is not reducible to the other forms addressed here (just as they are not reducible the one to the other). The overt emphasis in witnessing is on ethical rather than solely epistemic matters. The very idea of 'bearing witness' to teaching and teachers opens up fertile ground for *remembrance* in a policy era that seems in a headlong rush to abandon long-standing, profound educational values. One of these values is the significance of the person in the role of teacher, a truth which embodies, in turn, remembering that it is persons rather than roles who educate.[2]

The section that follows introduces the orientation of bearing witness that I enacted in the field-based study (and see Hansen, in press). The ensuing section elucidates the orientation through argument and illustration. In order to best capture the gestalt of bearing witness to teaching and teachers, I draw on field-notes from one teacher's classroom. I deploy these notes throughout the discussion as snapshots or sketches wherein the reader can observe my own witnessing. I do not claim to have succeeded in meeting the ethical and epistemic requirements of bearing witness. My hope is to make plain the contours and consequences of this orientation for educational work.

2. A witness to teaching and being a teacher

Let me begin with the following vignette drawn from my field notes.[3]

> Karolina and I were finishing a late morning walk in March in her K-5 school's immediate neighborhood. She had had a break in her teaching schedule, and had suggested we stretch our legs. As we wound up our conversation and stepped back through the old school building's heavy doorway, Karolina stopped abruptly and turned to me. 'Look, I know this is a research project and all that,' she said, 'but can I just ask: how am I <u>doing</u>? I mean, I really wonder if I am a good teacher with these children. If you have any suggestions for me, I'd really welcome them.' Karolina's tone of voice matched the sincere questioning in her eyes. She was not seeking flattery or easy comfort, nor was she requesting a battery of new classroom techniques. She wanted to know how she was faring—whether she was doing right by her students in both academic and moral terms.
>
> My response was immediate. 'You know your students, you've just been talking about them again on our walk. I've seen the many educational things you do with them individually, in groups, and as a whole class.' Karolina looked down for a moment. She gave her head a shake as she turned to lead us toward the stairway up to her classroom. Several adults and children were coming and going. She half-smiled, half-frowned, and said: 'Okay, well—I just don't know, you know?'

I did not anticipate Karolina's direct question that morning, with its vivid overtones of vulnerability and uncertainty. Her question startled me, on first hearing it, because she is an experienced, thirteen-year veteran in the profession whose work I had come to admire, and also because my self-assigned role in the endeavor did not include being a pedagogical adviser (see below). However, I did not stop to think before responding to her. I had done the thinking already through the hours I had spent in her classroom, the hours of conversation with her individually and with the larger group of teachers in the project, and the hours writing up my notes based on these encounters. I had seen that Karolina listens closely to her Grade 2 students and speaks with them mindfully. She is adept at picking out confused or frustrated voices amidst the lively cacophony that obtains during small group work. She places herself near the children during one-on-one tutorials, which are frequent in her classroom, while maintaining the dignity of space. Karolina *regards* her students. That is, she does not just monitor their external behavior, but looks at their doings with critical sympathy. She encourages the children and, without using the term in so many words, she expresses trust in them. When she addresses a child who is off task or disrupting another person, she does not insist they make eye contact with her. She manages the clock prudently as the class moves through the day's activities.

Karolina (who is a white woman in her 30s) sometimes misreads her students intellectually and emotionally, as she herself pointed out in our interviews. Some of her lesson activities do not connect with the class. She remarked on a number of occasions that she continuously seeks to improve her pedagogical techniques with regards to the subjects she teaches:

mathematics, writing, and reading. On a different platform, she also had much to say during our two years together about how tense her work environment has become under the current auditing system in American public education (cf. Sockett, 2012), with its testing and related standardizing imperatives. All of this comes on top of the very real challenges—and joys—she encounters teaching her 27 students, most of whom are first-generation Americans, who bring to the classroom varying and ever-changing degrees of academic readiness, social maturity, and general life experience.

Mindful of these complexities, the sense I increasingly had after each visit to her classroom (on eight different days all told) was that there was no better place for her students to be on a given weekday than with Karolina and their classmates. Karolina herself stated, more than once, that she could not imagine doing anything better with her days than teaching these children. By the time Karolina and I took our walk that March morning, and she asked about her teaching, I was in a position to respond as a witness.

This term pertains to something other than observing or cataloguing a teacher's behavior. Rather, it has to do with discerning expressions of the person in the role. Through the course of our ongoing interaction, I had come to see that Karolina *is* a person in her work as a teacher. This fact is both peculiar-sounding and elusive: peculiar because it is patently obvious she is a person, but elusive because this kind of truth is obscured—it is *not* treated as obvious—in much of today's research and policy environment in education. In today's zeitgeist, as touched on in the introduction, teachers are perceived as interchangeable 'parts' rather than as unique professionals who, with pertinent support and motivation, can contribute in distinctive ways to the education of children and youth, including from marginalized and immigrant groups in society who (at least in the US context) have often received unequal educational provision. Karolina and most of the other teachers in the undertaking I organized work directly with such young people. The teachers are purposive human beings: they bring to the classroom a serious pedagogical sensibility, a craftsperson's know-how, and an abiding sense of commitment that when *witnessed* makes it impossible to picture teachers as mere hired hands carrying out the dictates of others.

3. Witnessing as an ethical orientation in educational inquiry

The term 'orientation' differs in its emphasis from concepts like method, approach, or means. An orientation connotes embeddedness in the world. On the one hand, it points to how a person turns (or 'orients') the body in order to see and hear as best as possible. On the other hand, the concept spotlights how a person 'takes in' or 'receives' what is seen and heard. This 'turn' toward the world, implied in the idea of an orientation, incorporates aesthetic, epistemic, and moral dimensions that, with respect to bearing witness, come together in an umbrella notion of ethics. This notion of ethics is not new, though it is unfamiliar today. It is rooted in ancient sources as diverse as the writings of Plato, Confucius, and so-called Stoics such as Seneca, Epictetus, and Marcus Aurelius (Foucault, 2005; Hadot, 1995; Hansen, 2011; and see Higgins, 2011, who draws upon contemporary philosophical sources). The idea also emerges, both directly and indirectly, from more recent writers—all of whom were familiar with ancient texts—such as Michel de Montaigne, Marie de Gournay, Ralph Waldo Emerson, Friedrich Nietzsche, W. E. B. du Bois, and Virginia Woolf. In this dynamic tradition of thought and action, ethics denotes a form of mindful and emotion-full self-formation. It names an ongoing endeavor to cultivate as richly as possible one's intellectual, moral, and aesthetic capacities.

With respect to bearing witness to teaching and teachers, the aesthetic pertains to the inquirer's ability to discern and respond to beauty—or to gestures toward beauty—in the teacher's work. The inquirer needs to try to hold that beauty, which may come and go like a puff of wind, and keep it in sight long enough to render an account for others who care about the work. The intellectual dimension of witnessing has to do, on the one hand, with being a meticulous note-taker, juxtaposed, on the other hand, with an attempt to draw out lessons for educators if they take seriously the insights from the witnessing. Put another way, bearing witness to teaching and teachers has less to do with 'knowledge production', per se, and more to do with the pursuit of wisdom in research, policy, and practice. Wisdom is more capacious than knowledge, and in the best of worlds guides both the generation and uses of knowledge. As Epstein (2014) characterizes it: '[W]isdom is not a kind of thought so much as it is a thought-feeling, an alloy of the two. Wisdom is the result of the emotional saturation of thought and the intellectual saturation of feelings' (p. 205).

Intellectual and aesthetic capacities for witnessing merge with the moral. Here the concept moral differs from the ethical in that the former pertains to how the witness regards teachers: that is, whether he or she can bring to bear a critical sense of fairness, respect, and responsibility. This posture does not entail agreeing with or endorsing what is witnessed. It does not imply perceiving teaching through a romanticized or rose-colored lens. As mentioned previously with regards to phenomenology and portraiture, witnessing does not 'approve' or 'disapprove' of teachers. Rather, its moral dispensation is to *heed* teachers, to take them seriously in the fullest sense of that term (more on this point below). By comparison, ethics captures how the witness regards and treats her- or himself, not in an egoistic or narcissistic sense, but in the conviction that I must literally 'work on' myself if I am to cultivate my aesthetic, intellectual, and moral capacities—in short, if I am to ready myself to bear witness.

These remarks indicate why I referred in the introduction to witnessing as an ethical orientation in inquiry. Some further clarification will help elucidate the idea.

3.1. *Ethical proximity and witnessing*

A central condition for bearing witness to teachers and teaching is ethical proximity. This term refers to more than establishing a literal presence in the classroom and school. Ethical proximity constitutes a receptive relation with teachers, and a critical relation with oneself as a witness to their world. Ethical proximity obliges the researcher to work on her- or himself in the manner touched on above. Put another way, to bear witness requires something other than having at hand effective data-collection techniques, though these have an essential place. Rather, the posture calls upon the inquirer to try to do ontological justice to the teacher's presence: to try to perceive the person at play, the human being, rather than to remain on the behavioral surface which, in the nature of things, may appear highly conventional and predictable—so much so that I have heard colleagues remark how boring they find it to sit in on a classroom. To bear witness is never boring, though it is quiescent and requires patience. In bearing witness, every aspect of the inquirer's being is on call: his or her cognitive, aesthetic, and moral responsiveness. Anything short of this emotional and intellectual register may result in *objectifying* what is witnessed, when the point is to render its being, or what I dubbed a moment ago its presence.

Bearing witness, and the ethical proximity immanent within it, presumes it is worthwhile to listen to teachers and to spend time in their classrooms. The orientation presupposes that teaching is a holistic intellectual and moral practice in which the persons both students and teachers are becoming, through their interaction, are ever in formation as well as in question.[4] There are two reasons to highlight these presuppositions. One is that they are not shared by all teacher educators or researchers who examine aspects of the work. The other is that there are forces in operation in today's educational policy-making complex that would like nothing better, or so it appears, than to diminish as much as possible the autonomy teachers have in educating.

I presumed from the start of the study at hand that it would be worthwhile to bear witness to teachers and their work. This sense of worthwhileness can derive from multiple sources. In my own case, it stemmed from remembrance of good teachers I have had or who I know, reflections on my own work as a teacher and teacher educator, what I have learned from my previous research on teaching, and continuous study of research on teaching and on teachers' lives as well as teachers' own accounts of their work. My guiding aim in the endeavor was to be experientially and ethically *near* teaching: to be in teachers' classrooms, to talk with them in the school whenever time permitted, and to discuss with them, in the company of other serious-minded teachers, what it means to be a person in the world today and what it means to be a person in the role of teacher.

The witness in a classroom aspires to amplify the 'voice' of teachers and students, and to spotlight the 'look' of seemingly routine affairs. The aim in so doing is, in part, to persuade audiences who take a narrow view of teaching to re-evaluate their perception. This aim remains important because it is easy to miss or overlook daily activities and the significance they can embody. More strongly, it is possible to neglect these doings: to not attend, at all, to the 'quiet testimony' (cf. Goldberg, 2013) about what teaching means that is incarnated, for example, in a teacher's infinitely patient attentiveness to a child. In such cases, an aesthetic incapacity fuses with moral irresponsibility.

The witness heeds the fragile, evanescent, and yet also deeply substantive dimensions of teaching and learning. Put another way, the witness attends to deep human values at play in the everyday life of the classroom and school. The witness is dedicated to remembrance, understood not as conservative nostalgia but as an active, forward-looking state of mind in which cherished values—such as the dignity of every teacher and student, and the moral and intellectual significance of teaching—are *present* in thought and in action. The concern animating this article, touched on in the introduction, is that educational policy-making today lacks a sense of remembrance, overwhelmed as it appears to be by nationalistic, economic imperatives that privilege narrow forms of so-called accountability.

To set the stage for a closer look at ethical proximity and witnessing teaching, consider another vignette from my field notes.

> One morning in November, Karolina's students are engaged in Sustained Silent Reading (SSR), a practice that occupies the first 45 minutes or so of the day at every grade level in their K-5 school. Karolina's students have selected a book of their choice from the classroom library she maintains. The room is quiet as each child reads his or her text. Meanwhile, Karolina calls individuals up to her desk, one at a time, to review the 'realistic fiction'—a staple of the state-mandated academic requirements—that they are writing. The children choose topics, use multiple resources, and consult with Karolina regularly, while adhering to the state guidelines regarding the criteria of a successful piece of writing.

> One of the seven-year-old boys in the class, Jin, takes his seat next to her. A look of expectation and excitement crosses his face. Karolina begins to share her views and judgment of what he has composed. Jin listens intently, eyes wide open, looking up at her from time to time while she runs

a finger over the sentences on his page. He appears to be drinking in what she is saying, in large gulps triggered by his evident interest, curiosity, and perhaps pride. Karolina poses questions, too, and raises her head to gaze at him while he responds, his legs swinging under his chair, his body leaning forward with his hands grasping the seat. They go back and forth. At the end of their 10-minute-long consultation, Karolina remarks: 'That's some really great thinking! As you read on, you'll get more information to make up your mind further.'

Karolina appears to enter a distinctive pedagogical 'zone' during her one-on-one tutorials. She speaks with students patiently, quietly, and with enthusiasm. She sits near students but not too near, giving them space to move, gesticulate, bounce, shake their shoulders, and all the other things seven-year-old bodies do. She endeavors to create a meaningful conversation rather than simply speaking 'at' her students. She studs her comments with a refrain of questions designed to help them articulate themselves in the languages of writing, reading, and mathematics. 'And why did you do it that way?'—'Well, that was clever! How did you figure that out?'—'If this is what you want to do, what do you think you'll have to do next?'

In brief, Karolina enacts an intellectual and moral orientation in her work. She is respectful of the children, treating them as persons who have a mind and a heart. She is intellectually animated, encouraging them to approach the subject matter in a reflective and disciplined manner. She takes genuine pleasure in being with them. On more than one occasion during my visits, she would turn suddenly and swiftly to me, and with a wink would whisper 'This is the best job in the world!' or 'Isn't she amazing!' As she put it in an interview, when asked about why she has remained in the profession for 13 years:

> It's getting to spend time every day with a group of people that I really like ... I like the puzzle aspect of it [by which she means figuring out how best to help a student]. I like the interpersonal aspect of it. I like that I'm doing something that I feel good about at the end of the day, that I've made a positive contribution to the world. That feels really good. So it satisfies me emotionally, intellectually, spiritually. And it's fun. (I.6)

Karolina sometimes fails to find the right words, or the right strategy, for a child struggling in one way or another. According to her own testimony, she yearns to find 'the mental time' to think through fully what each of the 27 youngsters need on any given day. Her self-generated high standard—to try to reach each and every child, especially those with academic or emotional difficulties—fuels continuous uncertainty for her. She feels the paradox of teaching in the circumstances created by the system: the job is both possible and impossible. That fact calls to mind the frank question she posed to me on our walk touched on above.

However, there is an ontological dimension that carries the moral and intellectual aspects of Karolina's work. In a nutshell, Karolina allows her students to express their humanity. She creates conditions in which they are doing more than following, at a surface level, typical school routines. Rather, in Karolina's classroom they can enact their thinking, feeling, and wondering being. Karolina elicits the children's genuine thought as they express it in their terms as seven-year-olds. She draws out their authentic feeling for how they are faring: what they are doing well, what they are doing poorly, and what they hope to do. And she responds, if not in so many words, to their unspoken yet manifest desire to engage viscerally, rather than in a rote manner, the great, mysterious world represented by the written word, the spoken word, and the numeric realm, all of which they encounter every day in Karolina's classroom.

3.2. *Ethical proximity and witnessing as 'walking'*

Dustin and Ziegler (2007) provide an analogy, which I will extend here, that can further clarify the relation between ethical proximity with teachers and witnessing. The authors compare a botanist who enters a forest seeking a particular plant in order to study its morphology and medical potentialities, with a lover of forests who is not seeking any particular knowledge, as such, but rather a certain kind of reflective understanding. The botanist strides over countless species of flora and fauna in the quest to find the right plant. Put another way, the deeper the botanist penetrates the forest, the *less* he sees (Dustin & Ziegler, 2007, p. 40). In contrast, the walker takes her time. She is not *awaiting* something: namely, the sighting of a specific plant. Rather she is *waiting* (Heidegger, 2010, pp. 75, 76, *passim*). She is in no hurry. She takes things as they come. She notes the varied colors and textures of the life forms she encounters, the play of light and shadow as the sun's rays filter through the canopy above, and the sounds of birds, insects, and the wind through the trees. The walker also notes her responses to all this—to what Dewey (1988, pp. 15, 16) would call 'the immediate quality' of her experience, or her 'primary experience,' which is non-cognitive and saturated with aesthetic, emotional, and somatic elements. 'Secondary experience,' according to Dewey, denotes those phases in the walker's activity in which she attempts to interpret and explicate her primary experience.

The person's walk in the forest is a carefully undertaken endeavor. Put another way, the walker—like the botanist—brings to bear a critical mind respectful of the reality she seeks to engage.[5] The walker has a profound sense of purpose and well-wrought self-discipline. There is nothing casual or one-off about her walk, as if she were a tourist looking for novelty. The walker hungers, for example, for a deeper sense of what a forest *is* and what it *means*, both as an astonishing expression of life, and as an educator of the human being who aspires to grasp something about the ontology of existence, the 'why' she and the forest are here rather than solely the 'how' they are or 'what' they are. The walker moves as if 'called' by the forest. She follows its lead in her walk; she follows what it shows her while she is underway. She does not cling to a map or preset route; she does not try to control her steps in that manner. Instead, she practices—step by step by step—self-control, self-awareness, and attunement. She is both an eyewitness, attending to minute details, and an engaged I-witness, readying herself continuously to be receptive to the lessons of the forest.

Jean-Jacques Rousseau, Henry David Thoreau, and any number of other walkers attest to the philosophical power of giving oneself over to the forest (cf. Gilbert, 1991; Gros, 2014; Harrison, 2009; Robinson, 1989). These walker-writers and poets let the forest 'speak', as it were, rather than subject it to the silence of being a mere collection of objects to bag, dissect, and utilize. Many artists have put forward testimony about what it means to cultivate an ethical relation with the everyday world around us. For example, the painter André Marchand writes:

> In a forest, I have felt many times over that it was not I who looked at the forest. Some days I felt that the trees were looking at me, were speaking to me …. I was there, listening …. I think that the painter must be penetrated by the universe and not want to penetrate it …. I expect to be inwardly submerged, buried. Perhaps I paint to break out. (Merleau-Ponty, 1964, p. 167).

It merits adding that all that has been said about the walker in the forest can be said about the walker of cities—and of schools. As emphasized here, the walker is not looking *for* something pre-determined. The walker looks until, we can justly say, something looks back (Elkins, 1996).[6]

TEACHERS MATTER – BUT HOW?

In summary, ethical proximity entails cultivating a dynamic relation in which both world and self are in question. The witness's ways of knowing, perceiving, and understanding are not converted into a wedge to penetrate social reality. They are not put into the form of an objectifying hypothesis. Rather, the person's ways of knowing, perceiving, and understanding are opened up, not from an act of will as such, but through a careful, patient, and receptive orientation. In witnessing, to draw on terms from Jerome Miller, 'it is not we who break through to the unknown. It is the unknown which breaks through to us' (1992, p. 4).

In the undertaking at issue here, I sought to walk in the world of teachers at work. I endeavored to be near teaching and teachers in the critical and appreciative manner of a forest walker. I was not in search of particular expressions of the person, as if I were a botanist seeking a specific plant. Rather, I was interested in whatever expressions of the person in the role of teacher that I might be given to perceive—just as the walker moves in the quiet hope of encountering something that will speak of the 'why', of the grandeur, of the mystery, and of the pathos of life. As the months rolled by through the second year of field work, I became more practiced in what it means to wait, to be receptive and poised for what might be disclosed. The entire experience of the project has constituted an exercise in *readiness*: in readying myself to bear witness.

Late one morning in October, I am sitting in my usual corner spot in the classroom, near the long open closet where the children hang their coats and backpacks. The young people have just concluded their mathematics lesson. Karolina instructs them to form a line and prepare to go down the hallway for art class. I trail along behind. Karolina introduces me to the art teacher, Ms. Robertson, and I take a seat along a side wall. Karolina returns to her own classroom.

In a loud, officious voice that jars me at first, Ms. Robertson (a white woman in her late 50s or early 60s) demonstrates to the students how to cut out paper stars and shape them appropriately, this as part of putting together a paper representation of the sky. After providing her by-the-numbers directions, she tells the children to get to work, having already laid out supplies on the tables they're sharing.

In short order, however, it becomes evident that some of the students hadn't understood her directions. They look around uncertainly. Some copy what their peers are doing. Meantime, Ms. Robertson makes the rounds, pointing out particular materials and reminding individual students of what to do. As she approaches Kassim, he looks up at her with wide open but uncomprehending eyes. 'What's the matter,' Ms. Robertson asks him, 'don't you understand?' Kassim continues to look up at her. His face and searching eyes express a tremendous desire to understand, but also anxiety (he is still learning English, as I had discovered previously, and appears thrown by the art teacher's style, which is different from what he is accustomed to with Karolina). Ms. Robertson raises her voice, now almost shouting at Kassim about what to do, while he just keeps looking up at her, bewildered, anguished, and yet willing. He appears too nervous to utter a word.

Suddenly Harinder, another seven-year-old boy sitting across the room, says in a strong and steady voice, without looking up from the art materials in his hands: 'He doesn't understand you.' Ms. Robertson does a double-take, then repeats her directions to Kassim in a voice a few notches lower. As she does so, Kassim's neighbor, Ruby, turns to assist him with the task. Ms. Robertson had instructed the second graders to work independently, but does not interrupt Ruby: she senses the 'change' in the air. During this entire sequence, Harinder did not look up from his work, but went about his own business.

I had to leave the 60-minute art lesson a bit early, and on the way out of the building passed by Karolina's classroom. She was sitting at her desk. I gave her a brief report of what I had seen, mentioning how Harinder and Ruby had intervened when their classmate Kassim was stuck.

Karolina's face broke into a deep and serious smile. 'Oh, that's so wonderful to hear!' she said. 'That's how the children are with each other!' As I left the building, I pondered how the way they <u>are</u> with one another seems to mirror the way that she <u>is</u> when in their presence.

Karolina's 27 students are almost all the sons and daughters of adults who had immigrated to the United States (most of the children were born in the city where their school is located). Eight of the students have South American roots, nine South Asian, three East Asian, four Middle Eastern or African, and three Eastern European. Although they sometimes congregate in the classroom according to their families' regional origins, the children mingle fluidly with one another. They engage in paired or small-group activities in a cosmopolitan-minded manner that traverses rather than transcends (Saito, 2010, p. 334) ethnic, racial, and other markers of identity (Kromidas, 2011a, 2011b). They appear to find their cultural and individual diversity intriguing, exchanging spontaneously as well as at Karolina's urging various details about their families, backgrounds, and interests.

As the episode illustrates, and as Karolina observed, the students share an ethos regarding the way they 'are' with one another. For Harinder and Ruby, the two children who supported Kassim, their matter-of-fact intervention seemed as obvious a thing to do as walking with one foot in front of the other. It would require a full-blown account to track the emergence in their classroom of the sense of community that a witness can discern, with respect to the participants' mutual regard and their 'relational awareness' (Witte-Townsend & Hill, 2006, p. 13; and see Hansen, 1992). This sense is usually understated and yet palpable all the same. I did not 'discover' or 'uncover' this ethos. As a witness, as a person given over to the most receptive mode possible, it was disclosed to me in the moment of Harinder's and Ruby's conduct, along with many other moments in their classroom lives. Karolina and her students cast light, in a more than metaphorical sense, on what easily goes unseen. What increasingly stood out to me was how their classroom constitutes a place wherein their very personhood—their *being* as human beings—can appear and find expression. When Karolina and her students come to school, they are *coming to life* rather than leaving it behind.

As we have seen, that life is complex and presents endless demands on Karolina's attentiveness and responsiveness. An analogy can further illuminate this reality. Consider what is involved in responding to a compelling painting: taking in slowly and holistically its form, its substance, its style, and its provocation to thought and feeling. This endeavor is wondrous *and* exhausting, fulfilling *and* draining. Teaching children is not the same activity as appreciating paintings in the solitude, say, of a quiet gallery. But is teaching well any less draining? Nobody can perceive meaningfully 27 paintings in the same moment, much less the same hour or even day or week. But Karolina aspires to attend to 27 singular, non-interchangeable, irreproducible seven-year-old *persons*. She enacts everything she has learned in her 13-year-long career to realize that aim. But in other respects, judging from her testimony, the work strikes her as genuinely new every time she walks into her classroom.[7]

3.3. *Distance and nearness in witnessing*

Witnessing incorporates distance but not detachment from teaching and teachers. Detachment can imply objectification and aloofness. In contrast, distance implies—paradoxically, at first glance—what I have called ethical proximity. From start to finish in the endeavor described here, I conducted myself as someone who believes in the worthwhileness of teaching. As stated previously (p. 10 above), this posture does not imply endorsing what teachers do or approaching their work uncritically. I sought to embody the dimensions of witnessing addressed in this account: (1) being an eye-witness, which denotes faithfulness to fact and detail, (2) being an I-witness, implying ethical self-cultivation in order to be ready to bear witness in the aesthetic and moral terms adumbrated here, and (3) being an aye-witness, presuming from the start that 'yes' is the answer to the question whether teaching, in the depth senses so treasured by dedicated teachers, is worthwhile—which implies, in my view, being worth defending on the part of educational policy-makers.

When Karolina posed her question to me about her teaching at the close of our walk, I responded from a place of distance but not of detachment. Distance complements nearness. The one requires the other in order to be meaningful from an aesthetic, moral, and intellectual point of view. Recent work on classroom culture and education, undertaken from a cosmopolitan perspective, suggests that life in a classroom can be understood as a matter of coming closer and closer *apart* vis-a-vis others, while moving further and further *together* with them (Hansen, 2011, pp. 3–5, *passim*). As a teacher and group of students make their way through the school year, they learn more and more about one another. In one sense, they become 'closer'—but it is in fact closer and closer apart precisely because they come to see more clearly what makes each of them a distinctive, irreproducible human being, even if they may not use such terms to describe their experience. At the same time, they move further and further together into a universe of meaning represented by the subject matter they are studying and by their individual and collective engagement with it.

In likeness, in the endeavor at issue here the teachers and I also moved closer and closer apart—coming to see one another's distinctiveness—while also moving further and further together in our understanding of what is at stake in posing the questions about being a person that animated our work. Throughout this process, I judged it would be inappropriate to intervene in the teachers' work. I should not, for instance, co-construct classroom activities with them. For other scholarly undertakings, and for certain phases in teacher education, such doings are not only warranted but may be essential. However, I felt it crucial to maintain a posture as witness rather than as active participant, not because the latter would necessarily compromise my perception, but because I sought to respect in its totality the teachers' ethos. Put differently, though not a direct participant, indirectly I participated whole-heartedly by giving myself over to the occasion, as a scholar and person fully implicated in the contemporary trajectory of the practice of teaching. As the endeavor proceeded, the teachers and I spoke frankly about our views of teaching, of schools, and of educational policy. The two-year-long structure, comprising as it did extensive classroom visits, group discussions, and individual interviews, was indispensable for allowing this conversation to take form. The teachers responded to my witness by welcoming me, however preoccupied they were, whenever I came by their classrooms. We held countless conversations at the start or close of my visits. At every step of the way, I sought to heed the enactment of the person in the role of teacher.

People refer to 'self-consciousness', 'self-criticism', 'self-realization', and other related terms. But they do not typically use the term 'self-witness', and for sound epistemic and moral reasons. As I understand the concept, only another person can bear witness to my life—and, in order to do so, that person must bring critical sympathy to the endeavor rather than adopt a detached, clinical posture. It was important in the undertaking with teachers, and it remains so as I write these words, that I am an outsider to their singular pedagogical worlds. I am not *of* those worlds and am not trying to speak *for* them, which a witness is constitutionally unable to do because of the facts of distance (Adami & Hållander, 2015, p. 5). However, I do approach the teachers *from* a career-long immersion in the study and practice of teaching, as well as from an orientation of critical regard toward it (more on this in the conclusion). My status of being 'inside-the-practice' and 'outside-the-particular-classroom-world' does not blind me to the reality in teachers' work, but helps constitute the ground for my witness of it.

4. Conclusion: the importance of bearing witness for educational policy and research in the twenty-first century

The witness to teaching and teachers is in the throe of wonder and receptivity, rather than under the sway of a will to represent and explain. The witness does not add, at least directly, to our knowledge base of 'what works' from an instructional point of view. Teachers themselves, and subject-centered researchers, are the best source of such knowledge. Rather the witness aspires, among other things, to be a conduit for wisdom, to provide a channel or an occasion for its presence, as reflected in the root meaning of the term philosophy. The Greek words are *philia* and *sophia*—the love of wisdom. Wisdom and love are profound concepts, but are rarely touched on in mainstream educational research with its focus on knowledge and its applications. Perhaps this state of affairs reflects the fact that neither wisdom nor love constitute objects or possessions. They are not 'outcomes' that can be measured (at least without distortion), and they cannot be grasped directly. Yet wisdom and love are central to both witnessing and education.

Am I a good teacher with these children? That was the heartfelt and mind-felt question Karolina posed at the end of our walk one March morning. She meant something more than just whether she is 'effective.' Rather, she meant *good* as in goodness. She meant good as in her own rightness, her existential fitness, to be undertaking such a complex responsibility in the first place. Her fusion of heart and mind mirrors the element of love embedded in the very act of bearing witness as conceptualized here. This love carries the idea of the presumption of worthwhileness that I touched on previously to a higher platform. It calls upon the inquirer that much more from the point of view of ethics. It does so in the following way.

I referred previously to the forest walker as a lover of forests. Analogously, to bear witness to teaching and teachers brings the following questions to the surface. Does the inquirer *love* teaching, the possibilities in schools, and education itself enough to respond to teachers with adequate respect for the dignity and meaning of their vocation? Does the researcher love what teachers aspire to do—to teach—such that the researcher can learn to attend to the quiet testimony (Goldberg, 2013) in their work about the values in the practice? Does the researcher *feel* how infinitely challenging teaching is, and how vulnerable to failure and critique it renders its practitioners? Can the researcher approach teaching and teachers through reversing the order of terms in the concept 'understand'? That is, can I as a scholar learn to 'stand under' (Palmer, 1983, p. 67) rather than over, from an ethical, moral and epistemic point of view, the profoundly worthy object of love known as educating? Can I remember the fact that Karolina's doubts are not just her fears, but are the uncertainties that accompany teaching when it concerns itself with the actual persons alive in the school and classroom?

These challenging yet beckoning questions shed further light on why witnessing embodies distance but not detachment. Put another way, the questions point to why witnessing constitutes an ethical endeavor. As we have seen, the undertaking requires proximity, an ongoing process that encompasses work on the self in order be ready to bear witness (with readiness constituting no guarantees about what may ensue). The witness refrains from objectifying persons and things, and from assimilating them willy-nilly into preset epistemic categories. The witness elides the propensity of 'common sense' to categorize, package, or reject. Like other forms of inquiry, witnessing may yield counter-intuitive insights. Above all, the witness follows a sense of wonder and concern.

I began the endeavor characterized here with a sense of wonder regarding the unfathomable possibilities in teaching, and a sense of concern that current policy may be threatening the moral and intellectual integrity of those very possibilities. I believe there is a place on the larger horizon of educational research for the witness' inside/outside viewpoint. The witness may not add brand new knowledge, as such, to policy considerations. But the witness can remind those in a position to influence education of the necessity of wisdom, and of remembrance, in conducting such a profoundly human undertaking, in which the very persons we are and are becoming is at issue. The witness can help animate the conscience as well as consciousness of those in positions to lead, at whatever level of the system.

Bearing witness illuminates, in a fresh, vital way, the meaning of life in schools and classrooms. In so doing, it balances today's reform efforts with an equally significant agenda of conserving, in a reflective environmental sense of that term, dynamic questions such as what it means to be a person in the role of teacher and, indeed, what it means to educate in the first place. Without such questions, too many influential views may go unexamined, and too many important voices go unheeded.

Notes

1. For further details, see Hansen, Wozniak, and Diego (2015). The structure of the endeavor closely mirrored that of the Moral Life of Schools (MLS) Project, in which I had participated over 20 years previously (see Boostrom, 1994; Hansen, 2007; Jackson, 1992; Jackson, Boostrom, & Hansen, 1993). That structure—a dynamic combination of extensive fieldwork, group meetings, and individual interviews—allows the scholar, in my experience, *to begin again* in the most fundamental meaning of those terms. It positions the inquirer to move out from under the layers of interpretation that have settled upon the practice of teaching, and that can 'weigh it down' in the sense of making it difficult to look in fresh ways at its meaning and significance. The guiding question in the MLS Project was what it means to characterize teaching as a moral endeavor. My questions in the inquiry at hand here—about being a person including in the role of teacher—are closely related yet also more many-sided. As we will see, the concept of bearing witness emphasizes (a) the ethical dimensions of inquiry, with ethics constituting an umbrella concept that encompasses the moral, and (b) the centrality of critical remembrance in educational research, policy, and practice.
2. Buchmann (1985) memorably argued that teachers do not have the authority to pursue whatever 'personal' or idiosyncratic aims they wish, because teaching as a long-standing moral and intellectual practice has built-in obligations such as truthfulness about subject matter, commitment to student learning, patience with students, and more. I resonate with this perspective. But the role is not a blueprint. It constitutes an invitation and a challenge. The *person* must bring the role *to life* by metabolizing and enacting its dynamic elements, and no two persons will do so in the same manner.
3. By prior agreement, all names for participants in the article are pseudonyms.
4. I have sought to warrant this claim elsewhere (e.g. Hansen, 2001a, 2001b).
5. It is important to emphasize how appropriate it is, for some research purposes, to block things out in order to focus squarely upon a particular issue. Seeing 'less' can sometimes imply seeing

something well. I can picture the botanist and walker having a productive discussion along these lines. Indeed, the very same person—presuming he or she embodies the ecumenical epistemology—can be both botanist and walker.
6. For an example of how this perspective can enrich a teacher education program, see Hansen (2005).
7. I should add that if I had had the time to bear witness to the art teacher Ms Robertson's work—an undertaking which would have entailed multiple visits and considerable conversation—my remarks about her doings may have been rendered differently. As I plan to elucidate in a subsequent writing (I lack the space to do so here), witnessing as an orientation pertains, in principle, to interacting with any teacher, whether novice or veteran, successful or struggling.

Acknowledgements

The work reported herein has been supported by a grant from the Spencer Foundation, Chicago, Illinois, and by a Diversity Research Award from Teachers College, Columbia University. I am grateful to John Fantuzzo for his timely research assistance and thoughtful criticism. I thank the following people for generously offering their critical response to an earlier draft: Stefan Dorosz, Kevin Doyle, Jeff Frank, LeAnn Holland, Rachel Longa, Eric Shieh, and especially Cara Furman who provided pointed and insightful criticism. Finally, I appreciate Ana Cecilia Galindo Diego and Jason Wozniak for their sustained intellectual companionship as research assistants on the endeavor that is the source of this article.

Disclosure statement

No potential conflict of interest was reported by the author.

Funding

This work was supported by the Spencer Foundation and Teachers College, Columbia University.

References

Adami, R., & Hållander, M. (2015). Testimony and narrative as a political relation: The question of ethical judgment in education. *Journal of Philosophy of Education, 49*(1), 1–13.
Agamben, G. (2002). *Remnants of Auschwitz: The witness and the archive*. (D. Heller-Roazen, Trans.). New York, NY: Zone Books.
Barone, T., & Eisner, E. W. (2012). *Arts based research*. Los Angeles, CA: Sage.
Berlak, A. (1999). Teaching and testimony: Witnessing and bearing witness to racisms in culturally diverse classrooms. *Curriculum Inquiry, 29*, 99–127.
Boostrom, R. (1994). Learning to pay attention. *International Journal of Qualitative Studies in Education, 7*, 51–64.
Buchmann, M. (1985). Role over person: Morality and authenticity in teaching. *Teachers College Record, 87*, 529–543.

TEACHERS MATTER – BUT HOW?

Dewey, J. (1971). The study of ethics: A syllabus. In J. A. Boydston (Ed.), *John Dewey, the early works 1882–1898* (Vol. 4, pp. 219–362). Carbondale: Southern Illinois University Press.

Dewey, J. (1985). *John Dewey. The middle works 1899–1924: Vol. 9, democracy and education 1916*. (J. A. Boydston, Ed.). Carbondale: Southern Illinois University Press.

Dewey, J. (1988). *John Dewey, the later works 1925–1953: Vol. 1, experience and nature*. (J. A. Boydston, Ed.). Carbondale: Southern Illinois University Press.

Dewey, J. (1989). *John Dewey, the later works 1925–1953: Vol. 7, ethics*. (J. A. Boydston, Ed.). Carbondale: Southern Illinois University Press.

Di Paolantonio, M. (2015). Roger Simon as a thinker of the remnants: An overview of a way of thinking the present, our present …. *Studies in Philosophy and Education, 34,* 263–277.

Dustin, C. A., & Ziegler, J. E. (2007). *Practicing mortality: Art, philosophy, and contemplative seeing*. New York, NY: Palgrave Macmillan.

Eisner, E. W. (1976). Educational connoisseurship and criticism: Their form and functions in educational evaluation. *Journal of Aesthetic Education, 10,* 135–150.

Eisner, E. W. (1991). *The enlightened eye: Qualitative inquiry and the enhancement of educational practice*. New York, NY: Macmillan.

Elkins, J. (1996). *The object stares back: On the nature of seeing*. New York, NY: Harcourt Brace.

Emerson, R. W. (1983). *Emerson: Essays and lectures*. New York, NY: The Library of America.

Epstein, M. (2014). Lyrical philosophy, or how to sing with mind. *Common Knowledge, 20,* 204–213.

Felman, S., & Laub, D. (1992). *Testimony: Crises of witnessing in literature, psychoanalysis, and history*. New York, NY: Routledge.

Foucault, M. (2005). *The hermeneutics of the subject*. (F. Gros, Ed., & G. Burchell, Trans.). New York, NY: Picador.

Gilbert, R. (1991). *Walks in the world*. Princeton, NJ: Princeton University Press.

Goldberg, S. (2013). *Quiet testimony*. New York, NY: Fordham University Press.

Gros, F. (2014). *A philosophy of walking*. (J. Howe, Trans.). London: Verso.

Hadot, P. (1995). *Philosophy as a way of life*. (A. I. Davidson, Ed., & M. Chase, Trans.). Oxford: Blackwell.

Hansen, D. T. (1992). The emergence of a shared morality in a classroom. *Curriculum Inquiry, 22,* 345–361.

Hansen, D. T. (2001a). *Exploring the moral heart of teaching: Toward a teacher's creed*. New York, NY: Teachers College Press.

Hansen, D. T. (2001b). Teaching as a moral activity. In V. Richardson (Ed.), *Handbook of research on teaching* (4th ed., pp. 826–857). Washington, DC: American Educational Research Association.

Hansen, D. T. (2004). A poetics of teaching. *Educational Theory, 54,* 119–142.

Hansen, D. T. (2005). Creativity in teaching and building a meaningful life as a teacher. *The Journal of Aesthetic Education, 39,* 57–68.

Hansen, D. T. (2007). On seeing the moral in teaching. In D. T. Hansen, M. E. Driscoll, & R. V. Arcilla (Eds.), *To watch the water clear: Philip W. Jackson and the practice of education* (pp. 35–50). New York, NY: Teachers College Press.

Hansen, D. T. (2011). *The teacher and the world: A study of cosmopolitanism as education*. London: Routledge.

Hansen, D. T. (2012). W. G. Sebald and the tasks of ethical and moral remembrance. *Philosophy of Education, 2012,* 125–133.

Hansen, D. T., Wozniak, J. T., & Diego, A. C. G. (2015). Fusing philosophy and fieldwork in a study of being a person in the world: An interim commentary. *Studies in Philosophy and Education, 34,* 159–170.

Hansen, D. T. (In press). Among school teachers: Bearing witness as an orientation in educational inquiry. *Educational Theory*.

Harrison, R. P. (2009). *Forests: The shadow of civilization*. Chicago, IL: University of Chicago Press.

Hatley, J. (2000). *Suffering witness: The quandary of responsibility after the irreparable*. Albany: State University of New York Press.

Heidegger, M. (2010). *Country path conversations*. (B. W. Davis, Trans.). Bloomington: Indiana University Press.

Higgins, C. R. (2011). *The good life of teaching*. Hoboken, NJ: Wiley.

Hostetler, K. D. (Ed.). (1997). *Ethical judgment in teaching*. Boston, MA: Allyn & Bacon.

TEACHERS MATTER – BUT HOW?

Hostetler, K. D. (2011). *Seducing souls: Education and the experience of human well-being*. New York, NY: Continuum.

Jackson, P. W. (1992). The enactment of the moral in what teachers do. *Curriculum Inquiry, 22*, 401–407.

Jackson, P. W., Boostrom, R. E., & Hansen, D. T. (1993). *The moral life of schools*. San Francisco, CA: Jossey-Bass.

Kromidas, M. (2011a). Elementary forms of cosmopolitanism: Blood, birth, and bodies in immigrant New York City. *Harvard Educational Review, 81*, 581–606.

Kromidas, M. (2011b). Troubling tolerance and essentialism: The critical cosmopolitanism of New York City schoolchildren. In A. Lavanchy, F. Dervin, & A. Gajardo (Eds.), *Politics of interculturality* (pp. 89–114). London: Cambridge Scholars.

Lawrence-Lightfoot, S. (2005). Reflections on portraiture: A dialogue between art and science. *Qualitative Inquiry, 11*, 3–15.

Lawrence-Lightfoot, S., & Hoffman Davis, J. (1997). *The art and science of portraiture*. San Francisco, CA: Jossey-Bass.

Merleau-Ponty, M. (1964). Eye and mind. In J. M. Edie (Ed.), *Merleau-Ponty, the primacy of perception* (pp. 159–190). Evanston, IL: Northwestern University Press.

Miller, J. (1992). *In the throe of wonder: Intimations of the sacred in a post-modern world*. Albany: State University of New York Press.

Oliver, K. (2001). *Witnessing: Beyond recognition*. Minneapolis: University of Minnesota Press.

Palmer, P. (1983). *To know as we are known: Education as a spiritual journey*. San Francisco, CA: Harper & Row.

Peters, J. D. (2001). Witnessing. *Media, Culture & Society, 23*, 707–723.

Robinson, J. C. (1989). *The walk: Notes on a romantic image*. Norman: University of Oklahoma Press.

Ropers-Huilman, B. (1999). Witnessing: Critical inquiry in a poststructural world. *International Journal of Qualitative Studies in Education, 12*, 21–35.

Saito, H. (2010). Actor-network theory of cosmopolitan education. *Journal of Curriculum Studies, 42*, 333–351.

Santoro, D. A. (2011a). Teaching's conscientious objectors: Principled leavers of high-poverty schools. *Teachers College Record, 113*, 2670–2704.

Santoro, D. A. (2011b). Good teaching in difficult times: Demoralization in the pursuit of good work. *American Journal of Education, 118*(1), 1–23.

Santoro, D. A. (2013). 'I was becoming increasingly uneasy about the profession and what was being asked of me': Preserving integrity in teaching. *Curriculum Inquiry, 43*, 563–587.

Sherman, S. C. (2013). *Teacher preparation as an inspirational practice: Building capacities for responsiveness*. New York, NY: Routledge.

Simon, R. I. (2005). *The touch of the past: Remembrance, learning, and ethics*. New York, NY: Palgrave Macmillan.

Sockett, H. (2012). *Knowledge and virtue in teaching and learning: The primacy of dispositions*. New York, NY: Routledge.

Stillwaggon, J. (2016). The indirection of influence: Poetics and pedagogy in Aristotle and Plato. *Journal of Aesthetic Education, 50*, 8–25.

Van Manen, M. (1990). *Researching lived experience*. Albany: State University of New York Press.

Van Manen, M. (2014). *Phenomenology of practice: Meaning-giving methods in phenomenological research and writing*. Walnut Creek, CA: Left Coast Press.

Wills, J. S., & Sandholtz, J. H. (2009). Constrained professionalism: Dilemmas of teaching in the face of test-based accountability. *Teachers College Record, 111*, 1065–1114.

Witte-Townsend, D. L., & Hill, A. E. (2006). Light-ness of being in the primary classroom: Inviting conversations of depth across educational communities. *Educational Philosophy and Theory, 38*, 373–389.

Zembylas, M. (2006). Witnessing in the classroom: The ethics and politics of affect. *Educational Theory, 56*, 305–324.

Global injustice, pedagogy and democratic iterations: some reflections on why teachers matter

Elaine Unterhalter

ABSTRACT

The article argues teachers matter because of their potential to engage in critical reflection on values associated with connecting the local, the national and the global. Their practice can support those who are dislocated, and who have no place. Teachers matter because they can help us understand how we share humanity and aspirations across many differences. The discussion identifies some similarities between approaches to pedagogy and Seyla Benhabib's notion of democratic iteration. Both concepts suggest a navigation between the general, the particular and some of the complexities of their contradictions which can guide teachers' work. Frameworks from cosmopolitanism and the capability approach are explored for detail they provide on how this navigation can be considered in practice across differently politically constituted formations and diverse, unequally situated groups. Drawing on some reflections on work in an international classroom, the conclusion explores some of these navigations across inequalities.

How do teachers matter in a world marked by inequality, injustice and many failures of our attempts to institutionalize global human rights frameworks and address poverty? What aspects of these issues should teachers teach, and how should they do so? If the space for reflection on these difficult problems is narrowing, because of the parochial nationalisms associated with public testing regimes, and particularly limited understandings of educational accountability, what should teachers do? How can they help build insights to guide wiser ways forward when the process of education reform in so many countries has come to focus on a very limited set of national, often primarily economic outcomes, with teachers often highly regulated to deliver on these? If pedagogy is made a mechanical set of skills to develop a narrow range of learning outcomes, what space is open in formal education to reflect on global injustices that touch all our lives?

This article approaches this problem by outlining a working definition of pedagogy that makes space for engaging with global injustice and inequalities. It draws on ideas about democratic iteration developed by Benhabib (2006, 2011) to explore complex processes of public argument in relation to understanding rights, issues of sovereignty, exclusion and transnationalism. These political processes are linked with pedagogic relationships, and woven into a definition of pedagogy. Frameworks for addressing international inequalities drawing on cosmopolitanism, capabilities and features of equity are deployed to show how they can provide some of the organizing ideas for the critical reflection on values associated with democratic iteration. In the concluding section, some practices of doing this in an international higher education classroom are presented as one riposte to the parochial nationalism of test driven cultures in education.

The argument is organized in four parts. It begins with some definition regarding pedagogy, the situatedness of teachers and links their ethical engagements addressing inequalities with the notion of democratic iteration. In the second section, some frameworks to engage the question of global injustice are presented. This includes some discussion of the potential associated with concepts of cosmopolitanism (Brock, 2013a), the capability approach (Nussbaum, 2011; Sen, 1999) and the concept of equity. This selection is by no means the full range of concepts open to us in thinking about global inequalities, pedagogies and how teachers matter, but the combination has been selected as a preliminary framework which appears generative for articulating some of the values associated with pedagogies around global injustice. In the third part some vignettes of practice are presented. These are drawn from experience working in a university on education inequalities in a globally connected world, reaching across locales and struggling to develop understanding. They consider how the frameworks and pedagogic practices connect and some of the navigations they entail. The conclusion revisits the nature of the problem of what teachers can do caught between a highly regulated education system, and the staggering inequalities and injustices of the contemporary world. It attempts to mark out a terrain for practice, which draws on democratic iteration and suggests as a starting point gaining insight through critical reflection on global injustices drawing on frameworks, such as cosmopolitanism and the capability approach, which allow space for the discussion of values, diversity and teachers' agency.

Pedagogic relations and democratic iteration

The definition of pedagogy in particular national contexts draws on histories of educational thought, experiences with the establishment of education systems and accounts of teachers' work. However, a single definition of pedagogy is controversial. Recently, the position of some countries in global league tables of education outcomes have led to the branding and export of particular pedagogic styles, and the critique of others (Auld & Morris, 2014; Morris, 2015). Alexander (2008, pp. 45, 46) notes how much the discussion of pedagogy by policy-makers in England from the 1980s, tilted the axis away from teaching to learning. Young (2012, 2013) has argued for the centrality of understanding the social relations of knowledge in analysing learning in a globalizing world, linking pedagogy with knowledge and curriculum. Moore (2012), charts the focus of much teacher education in the UK on specific skills, discourses of charisma and the invocation of reflective practice as a catchall to deal with a wide range of difficulties and experiences. Garrison (1997) highlights a different side of the coin of pedagogy concerned with love and wisdom. In meditating on the success of the Finnish education system in PISA tests over the last 10 years, Sahlberg (2011) reflects on the high values given to Finnish teachers' own extensive education and agency. These different approaches highlight how difficult it is to capture a single definition of pedagogy. Alexander suggests one which will underpin the analysis in this article, because it seeks to situate any definition of pedagogy both nationally and internationally. It combines aspects of practice, with consideration of knowledge, research and a range of values, all of which seem highly pertinent to considering what informs teachers' engagements with global injustice and inequality. Alexander (2008, p. 47) defines pedagogy as

> The act of teaching, together with its attendant discourse of educational theories, values, evidence and justifications. It is what one needs to know, and the skills one needs to command, in order to make and justify the many different kinds of decision of which teaching is constituted.

This definition entails appreciating practice and reflections on day-to-day experience. It underscores how these are informed by particularly situated views of education policy, history, research and understandings of knowledge. It acknowledges practice is animated by a range of values, which may be local, national or global in particular mixtures. Running through this definition is a sense of pedagogy mediating features of the work of teachers that stand between the general and the particular, the historical, contextual and everyday agency. It is this dynamic that appears generative in thinking about how teachers matter in relation to developing understandings of global injustices and inequalities.

This reverberation between the general and the particular in the definition of pedagogy echoes a central notion in Benhabib's work concerned with democratic iteration. Benhabib (2011, p. 15) develops the concept of democratic iteration to convey

> how the unity and diversity of human rights is enacted and re-enacted in strong and weak public spheres, not only in legislatures and courts, but often more effectively by social movements, civil society actors, and transnational organisations working across borders.

She, thus, uses the concept to navigate between concerns with the general and the particular. A definition of pedagogy, such as that used by Alexander, is similarly situated in the public sphere of the school, but also entails a range of enactments across borders, between learners, teachers, families, civil society, knowledge communities and various kinds of transnational network. Attempts to enact some integrating but self critically constructed 'unity', acknowledging this diversity, makes up some of the texture of what teachers do, and one of the reasons they matter.

Democratic legitimacy, Benhabib (2011, p. 74) argues, drawing on the work of Habermas and the Frankfurt School, rests on the existence of institutions and the processes available for discursive reflection on those institutions. Thus, the legitimacy of ideas about rights, equalities or social justice would derive both from national or cross-national institutions, which establish these, and from practices of critical review. Pedagogic relationships rest on the existence of education systems, and, either formally or informally, in everyday practice they may provide opportunities for reflection on these processes. However, the extent to which critical reflection is encouraged or supported varies considerably across contexts. Whether or not there are opportunities for reflection and discussion of local, national or global injustices is also highly dependent of the contexts in which different teachers work.

Benhabib (2011, p. 75) sees democratic iterations as 'processes of interplay between democratic will and opinion formation, on the one hand, and constitutional principles on the other hand'. Thus, pedagogic relationships, for example, as outlined by Young (2012) mediating between different forms of knowledge, reflecting both on institutional conditions and the situatedness of learners and teachers, are part of democratic iterations. Pedagogic relationships, in acknowledging forms of knowledge that derive both from disciplines, institutions, individual situation and the interplay between them, resonate with some of the key moves associated with the process of democratic iteration. Benhabib (2011, p. 12) argues that the right to have rights can be established through a justificatory universalism, which has the potential to be 'non-essentialist, non-reductionist and deeply imbricated in the democratic project'. Part of this process of establishing justificatory universalism acknowledges a generalized notion of the other and a concretely situated engagement with particular others (Benhabib, 1995, 2011). This two-sided notion resonates with some of the discussion of what is entailed in thinking about pedagogies and how to mediate between forms of knowledge codified in disciplines at a general level and generated in situations or experiences at the level of the particular teacher or student . It also addresses some of the issues of the general and the particular in the enactment of care or reflections on rights and inequalities.

For Benhabib (2006, p. 67), democratic iterations entail a dialectic of rights and identities in the process of which the meanings of identities and rights claims are 'reappropriated, resignified, and imbued with different meanings'. On many pressing contemporary global issues there are no simple agreements. For example, there are markedly divided views on immigration, and no easy solutions are on the table regarding the millions of refugees and migrants, now exceeding the numbers at the end of the Second World War. Ignatieff (2014) has characterized the current period as presenting a new world disorder, in which authoritarian regimes used the supercharged markets of capitalism to strengthen economic growth and curtail political opposition. When the economies built through these processes contract, as they have done dramatically since the end of 2015, there is a turbulent political fallout, in which established institutions are called into question (Mason, 2016; Piketty, 2016). Under these conditions the form of democratic iteration that seeks to understand both the relationship of things and the disputed frames through which people interpret them, requires particularly alert pedagogical practice. Teachers matter because they are well placed to learn both what is and be alert to a range of values to interpret this empirical world. In the next section, I suggest a number of approaches drawn from cosmopolitanism and capabilities that could be useful in this process of engaging with global injustice and steering between different networks of obligation and different kinds of understanding of inequality.

Cosmopolitanism and capabilities: diverse obligations, equalities and forms of equity

While there are a number of discussion of how teachers approach global injustice, for example, drawing on ideas about global citizenship or development education (Andreotti, 2015; Marshall, 2009), I have focused this discussion on some of the texture provided by the concepts of cosmopolitanism and the capability approach for thinking about these issues, as both have engaged the question of diversity, the general and the particular in different ways. Thus, theorizations of cosmopolitanism have engaged with the question of scale in relation to understanding what duties we owe to people who are not citizens of the same country in the context of a globalizing world, where boundaries of nation states matter enormously in some areas, and very little in others (Harvey, 2013). Writers working with the capability approach have considered the question of how to engage the question of diversity, and many changing contexts, which has particular relevance for the wide range of situations in which teachers work daily under historical conditions of uneven globalizations. Their analysis focuses on the relationships between opportunities (capabilities) and what comes to realized (functionings), echoing the arc of connection made by the notion of pedagogy. I now want to unpack the ideas of cosmopolitanism and the capability approach a bit further in relation to some of the dynamics associated with pedagogies confronting global injustice and inequalities.

Cosmopolitanism is a term much contested. On the one hand, it is used to describe a globalized elite, who have fashioned a world of free trade, information flows, widening inequalities, the consumption of luxuries and positional goods, and used state and international institutions to further a 'duty free' culture that pays scant attention to the particularities of conditions on the ground (Harvey, 2013). On the other hand, the term is also used in political philosophy to try to deliberate on the question of whether we owe anything above a bare minimum of ensuring rights to survival to people who are not citizens of the same country. A rich literature has developed on how to think about cosmopolitanism as a response to global injustices and forms of inequality (eg Brock, 2013a; Rovisco & Nowicka, 2013) and to some extent this has been taken up in work on education, both positively (Hansen, 2011; Hayden, 2013) and doubtfully (Harvey, 2013; Popkewitz, 2012). Hansen (2011) has associated cosmopolitanism with teaching in schools and some of the processes of moving together and apart that meld the global and the local. Starkey (2012) outlines some principles of a shared humanity associated with rights and cosmopolitan utopias. Some feminist versions look beyond the sovereignty of states and develop notions that link recognition of vulnerability, and an ethics of care and mourning (Butler, 2010) or responsibilities across global lines of association (Young, 2011) .Others identify forms of subaltern cosmopolitanism that link together experiences of dispossession (Zeng, 2014). Some identify cosmopolitanism as a term whose meaning is struggled over, with situatedness and contradiction comprising major areas of contestation (Schiller & Irving, 2014). Benhabib (2011) links cosmopolitanism with democratic iterations and critical reflections on national and transnational frameworks of rights and wider formal notions of obligation. It can be seen that cosmopolitanism, shares with Alexander's definition of pedagogy a dynamic of stretching between the universal and the particular. Some writers problematize this, while others deny its significance.

All the work on cosmopolitanism, as an investigation of obligations enacted juridically or pedagogically, considers the question of how we practice connection across a general idea of rights, responsibilities and vulnerability. This work acknowledges there is a distinction between what we construct as abstract and particular, and some of the astute discussion (Moellendorf, 2013; Valentini, 2013) draws out how important it is to make distinctions.

Thus, part of teachers' pedagogical work entails thinking about the space occupied by the local, the national, the global, their intermixture and the terrain between drawing on some of the ideas the cosmopolitan debate has generated about moral equality, forms of national and global belonging, the rights held by the poor and responsibilities beyond borders (Schiller and Irving 2014; Brock, 2013b). The debate around cosmopolitanism between supporters and critics, gives content to a pedagogy that can help to place ourselves and our relationships on a map of critically examined values. One feature of this might entail understanding how these boundaries are experienced by those who are dispossessed or delegitimized. Another might comprise distilling how experiences of pain and loss are articulated and understood in a world of marked inequalities. A third might constitute appreciating the power play and contestation operating in international relations at different levels. Diverse curricular spaces or moments in a day of teachers' work open different terrains. How is this diversity of spaces to be navigated? The capability approach, as a method of analysis gives some pointers.

TEACHERS MATTER – BUT HOW?

The capability approach gives a central focus to human diversity, and the link between opportunities or capabilities, and functionings, that is valued 'doings and beings' (Nussbaum, 2011; Sen, 1999). Capabilities can be more flexible than rights in thinking about inequalities in diverse local, national and global settings. Diversity takes many forms, highlighting both multiple contexts, but also a range of different kinds of inequality. Sen's (1980) famous question was initially posed in relation to inequality of what. Stewart (2000) has outlined vertical and horizontal inequalities, which I have referred to as concerned with the inequality of whom (Unterhalter, 2015a). I have also identified a third facet of thinking about inequality in education, which I have termed an engagement with the inequality of how, which I see as a particular feature of pedagogy (Unterhalter, 2015a).

Sen's classic work (1992), posed the question regarding the value of equality. If we are to distribute benefits and burdens between people equally, as we all share the planet, what dimensions of people's lives should be compared in order to establish whether one person is worse off than another? Sen answered we should not simply equalize resources, or utility, but rather capabilities, opportunities and a connection between means and ends. This answer highlights a very significant role for teachers and pedagogic relationships. In defining inequality of what in terms of Sen's notion of capabilities we are looking, not simply at resources, or amounts, that is number of years of education or to what level someone can read, do mathematics or achieve in PISA tests. We are comparing what opportunities people do or do not have to fulfil what it is they have reason to value. Teachers matter partly because they may help ameliorate unequal national or global division of resources or guide reflections on what people want. They may offer opportunities to understand a world of injustice and inequality and engage critically with the institutions which form that.

A second feature of inequality and global injustice concerns inequality of whom. Stewart (2009) has distinguished between what she calls vertical and horizontal inequalities. Vertical inequalities concern what is distributed, for example, education or work opportunities or outcomes. She contrasts these with horizontal inequalities, which exist between groups constructed on the basis of race, ethnicity, gender or class. Horizontal inequalities often attach to ideas such as religious beliefs, cultural or political or gender values. They are often deep-seated, intersecting and work at levels that are both rational and emotional. The bodies, feelings and emotions of one group are lauded, and those of another reviled. A troubling aspect of horizontal inequalities is the depth of the hatred, racism, misogyny, xenophobia or violence, that can be passed down over generations. Indeed it may be that the formal structures of an education system do not officially admit these forms of inequality, but informal processes, associated with neighbourhoods, friendships, marriage and intra-generational belonging, maintain these inequalities making redress of vertical inequalities particularly complex. Vicious words exist in just about every language for women who do not conform sexually or intellectually. Women's bodies and forms of dress often demarcate the boundaries of belonging within nations and in transnational migrant communities (Anthias, 2008; Anthias & Yuval-Davis, 1993; Yuval-Davis, 2011; Yuval-Davis & Anthias, 1989). These hatreds also attach to men from subordinated groups, and are often phrased in terms of insults around sexuality.

To signal some of the ways this expands Sen's discussion of inequality the question Stewart is concerned with may be phrased as inequality among whom. This raises questions of how to craft pedagogic relationships to breach silences, unravel some of the assumptions around identities and violence and review intersecting inequalities. All these processes suggest in-depth pedagogic work by teachers that engages the complexity of democratic iterations.

TEACHERS MATTER – BUT HOW?

Teachers are crucial transmitters of ideas about horizontal inequalities. They are also key actors in helping to unpick the forms in which they are constructed and reproduced. Pedagogic relationships may use instruction, appropriately sequenced or scaffolded disciplinary knowledge, other forms of reflection on information and experience, or some combination. One of the problems around advancing insight into this area is the gaps in our knowledge, and the ways in which academic knowledge is often out of step with the lived experiences of inequality. This begs questions about professional distance, dispassionate evaluation, how we gather information, make connections and judgements. How teachers address the inequalities of whom, has been documented in particular areas concerned with race, gender, ethnicity or disability, but much work needs to be done on considering these intersections.

A third form of inequality, not covered by the geometric notions of vertical and horizontal inequality, talks to education as a site of process and practice and I have termed this aspect of diversity a consideration of the inequality of how (Unterhalter, 2015a). This form of procedural inequality sets in place particular kinds of hierarchies between, for example, teachers and learners, which overlay the inequalities of distribution and recognition associated with horizontal and vertical inequalities. Education is a site of many procedural inequalities. For example, it encodes differences of age, most evidently between adults and children, but also between children of different age groups, and in higher education between older and younger academics. In all phases, there are inequalities across hierarchies of employment and decision-making. There are inequalities in educational experience and resources, given the vast differences between institutions working in the same phase. There are inequalities between formal and informal knowledge areas, between the status of disciplines and research methodologies, forms of curricular knowledge and in the regard given to empirical and theoretical accounts of particular problems, such as global injustice. There are inequalities between teachers regarding the severity of the regulatory regimes they are subject to, and between approaches to curricula that compel conformity and those that encourage deliberation. Curriculum selection is associated with inequality of how. Thus, the identification of powerful knowledge, how this is organized, sequenced and evaluated contributes to this form of inequality. The democratic iterations I have linked with pedagogy require some naming of these inequalities of how, and pedagogies which engage them entail some thoughtful practices to navigate across these divisions, unequal locations and relationships, considering both the universal and the particular.

What are the processes through which these different facets of inequality can be navigated, and addressed pedagogically? Equity is a term which, together with cosmopolitanism, can illuminate some of the ways teachers can engage in pedagogic relationships which address different kinds of global inequalities. To illustrate some possibilities I draw on some work I have done looking at the changing meanings of equity in English (Unterhalter, 2009). The semantic history of the word equity and the social contexts in which it was deployed, indicate three different ways to think about its meanings. Each has particular implication for thinking about pedagogic relation. In its earliest form equity signalled an association between the powerful and the powerless, that accorded each equal moral worth, and signalled processes of participation in knowledge formation and joint learning. I have termed this equity from the below (Unterhalter, 2009, p. 417). In a later incarnation equity signalled the establishment of special courts that were neither the domain of the church nor the nobles, but regulated both. I have termed this equity from above (Unterhalter, 2009, pp. 418,

419). In the age of capitalism equity came to mean money or forms of capital and I have termed this equity from the middle (Unterhalter, 2009, p. 421).

Equity from above delineates how we might establish institutions nationally or transnationally, which secure people's rights to say health, education or livelihoods, facilitate fair forms of distribution, taking account of contexts of intersecting inequalities, but primarily addressing inequality of what and inequality of whom. This seems particularly appropriate to use in evaluating curricula used in teacher education and the extent to which they provide a scaffolding of ideas which address adaptive preference, and the form of inequality of what that makes it difficult for children in absolute poverty to articulate what it is they have reason to value (Unterhalter, 2012). Equity from above is also important in putting in place laws or institutional forms for schools or teacher education colleges which work to undo racism or gender discrimination, associated with horizontal inequality. But, we know through a host of studies, that making the institutional form will not in and of itself address the kinds of practice that perpetuate inequalities. This needs a different level of engagement. Equity from above seems to have affinity with a form of social justice cosmopolitanism concerned to develop the transnational institutions that can oversee or support the securing of rights, when national systems fail or are weak. This form of equity from above seems well suited to address some transnational monitoring of processes to secure equality of rights and some, but not all capabilities, possibly those linked with aspects of gender or forms of resource inequalities.

Equity from below is particularly attentive to forms of participation, mediating the relationships of the powerful and the powerless. I think this form of equity talks to engagements with inequality of how and inequality of whom in schools, classrooms and lessons. It looks at processes by which learners and teachers are positioned in relation to particular forms of knowledge, pedagogic practice, how exclusions might be challenged, and inclusion addressed, how the multidimensionality of inequality, and particular registers around violence are understood and learners and teachers helped to confront and transform this (Parkes, 2015). Equity from below evokes forms of subaltern cosmopolitanism, and it may be that the democratic iterations associated with pedagogic relationships can help with listening to silences, disentangling particular themes, of pain and exclusion, although this requires time and space to secure.

I have linked equity from the middle with flows of money, technologies, expertise and ideas, which enable equity from below to articulate with equity from above. Equity from the middle appears particularly salient in connecting the concern with the three different kinds of inequality (of what, of whom and of how) which I outlined. Teacher education, teacher deployment, teacher communication, conditions of work, teacher agency and professional ethics, are all instances of equity from the middle that need to engage with diversity and ways of linking the general and the particular. Hansen (2011) has written about the ways in which people engage with reading the world, encouraging practices in classrooms that are at once global and local, expanding the scope of both. Democratic iterations and pedagogic relations depend on further theorizing these processes in the middle. Pedagogic relationships of democratic iteration rest both on processes from below, but also on building and supporting teachers to attend to transnational processes of securing rights, building frameworks of care and circulating information about dispossession. In a recently completed study with newly qualified teachers in five Nigerian states, it is evident how little support young people entering teaching have had to understand the local, national or global contexts of the teaching skills they are given (Unterhalter, 2016).

An important area for critical engagement with equity in the middle is the terrain of measurement, where there are opportunities both to use existing forms of measurement, like PISA, to reveal some of the inequalities of what and inequalities of whom, as well as critical discussion of how we might better construct measures of equality in education that consider some of the features of inequality of how as it plays out across global, national and local sites through gender relations (Unterhalter, 2015b), disabilities or other injustices (Klees & Qargha, 2014). This suggests the importance of investigating how vertical, horizontal and procedural or pedagogic forms of inequality interconnect, and what this entails for the work teachers currently do and could be supported to do better. We need to investigate how or whether teachers' negotiations between different kinds of inequalities bridge aspects of the public and private, the analytical and experiential, the content of knowledge areas and the formation of particular dispositions, and what supportive indicators of this process might be. What resources do teachers have to look at the roots of local, national and global inequalities and their connection? We have very few studies of this in practice, but I surmise that where this happens there are particularly in-depth pedagogic encounters associated with well supported teachers, explicitly engaged with considering inequalities.

In this section, I have explored some of the potential associated with the ways scholars of cosmopolitanism have tried to sort out the question of how we understand our relationships of general and particular obligation. I have also discussed how some of the appreciation of context, and different forms of inequality in the discussion of the capability approach, generates interest in features of equity and democratic iteration, that give content to the notion of how teachers matter. Teachers matter because they reflect critically on the education, political and social systems in which they are located, and have some potential to engage with the inequalities of what, of whom and of how, addressing relationships that are top-down, bottom-up and through the middle. In the next section, I reflect on some of my own practice in an international classroom, trying to draw out some of the pedagogic relationships that are in play, highlighting some of the ways that thinking about teaching matters.

Some pedagogic relationships in a transnational classroom

I have worked for 25 years with a diverse student body at the Institute of Education, University of London (now University College London, Institute of Education) teaching on masters courses I have selected four learning moments to evoke some of the complexity of pedagogic relationships associated with global injustices and have tried to draw out how some features of cosmopolitanism, democratic iteration and capabilities are at play, and why teachers matter.

The setting is a university which provides considerable support for students. Excellent library and information services, experienced teachers and administrators and articulate peers combine with London as a global city and a resource in itself. But these advantages are mediated. The university provides benefits because fees are high. Staff experience rests on combinations of teaching and research which impose boundaries of time and space on the pedagogic relationships that can develop. Students and staff bring to the classroom divergent experiences with and perspectives on intersecting structures of inequality regarding race, ethnicity, gender and class. Agreements are not pre-given. Differences in language, access to cultural and other forms of capital can separate students from each other and from their teachers. London as a global city is linked as much with the injustices associated with slavery and the expansion of capitalism, as it is with the growth of equalities and struggles for justice. Thus, in practice as a teacher one has many tasks. Some entail bridging the differences between learners, between any particular learner and oneself, and the interpretation of the curriculum different learners make. Other tasks entail a scaffolding of a critical reflection on where we are in time and space, with the knowledge we are reviewing. We are also engaged in ensuring some insight into the inequalities of opportunities in education round the world and how to confront them. The democratic iteration in the classroom is one that entails moving between the concrete particular, and the generalized frame.

The mission statement for the section of the department in which I work, frames our practice in terms of an engagement with 'the protection and advancement of rights and capabilities in education at all levels' (Education & International Development, 2013). We are concerned with preparing students 'to become competent, confident and critical professionals who can analyse education and related policy, research and practice issues at a high level of analytical rigour with appropriate regard to context'. The instances I present below are ones where engagements with global injustice were almost beyond words and academic frameworks. In these four vignettes the pedagogic relationships evoke searching in a world that is simultaneously striving for forms of order and connection, as epitomized by research and teaching, yet is also disordered, unravelling, difficult to describe, increasing inequalities, injustices and disorganizing pedagogic projects. In teachers trying to reflect on this, they make a space in which it is clear that what they do matters.

Miwako Tokuda, was born on Okinawa, a Japanese island invaded by American troops at the end of the Second World War. The trauma of that time was intense. As the Americans advanced, Okinawan families were instructed by the military hierarchy that they should kill themselves, rather than risk dishonour through capture. Many complied. Miwako's grandfather and some aunts survived. She wanted to interview them to explore memory, gender and catastrophe. But the pain of doing so was too acute. Her dissertation *Someone is listening* (Tokuda, 2005) was an attempt to try to work out what this silence might mean for teaching and learning about extreme events. The work was developed through many conversations between me and Miwako, and between Miwako, members of her close family and some of her classmates.

Kay Andrews, a specialist in teaching in schools about the Holocaust in Europe, wrote her Masters dissertation on some of the silences in Holocaust education about gender, linking this with ways in which memorials to the genocide in Rwanda have remembered and forgotten women (Andrews, 2013). She grappled with how to evaluate intersecting injustices, and bring this learning into thinking about how to memorialize genocides across different settings. She worked with an extensive body of written scholarship on this theme, her conversations with colleagues and her dialogues in supervision with me.

A student revealed to me that he had been a child soldier in the Biafran war in the 1960s. Now a well-established professional in the UK, he was keen to understand education and international development. I hoped his experiences would provide some unique perspectives on the literature on child soldiers. But the compressed time frame of a short module distorted our pedagogic relationship and seemed to get in the way of learning. The literature on child soldiers is written from the outside, while his experiences and memories were complex requiring many layers of exploration. I failed to help him make connections.

TEACHERS MATTER – BUT HOW?

Lucky Omaar, studied for her MA after travels between Somalia, Kenya, the USA and the UK, experiencing the pains and upheavals of the Somali diaspora. While working on her dissertation (Omaar, 2015) with young Somali women, living in Kenya, terrible atrocities perpetrated by Al Shabab took place. Was there a place for reflections on these events in the dissertation, or was our pedagogic relationship to be structured by keeping to academic timetables and formal lines of reflection? Lucky and I discussed this extensively, and she also reflected with other students, academic and administrative staff and her networks in Kenya.

I have selected these four examples because they highlight features of injustices and inequalities of our contemporary world, the legacies of colonialisms, wars, the difficulties and silences for those who survive. They point to the complexity of pedagogic relationship suggesting the difficulties of teaching and learning in a global classroom, trying to listen to silenced and oppressed voices and some of the achievements of expanding understanding through in-depth work and the wide range of networks that support this teaching. They distil some of the concerns of the cosmopolitanism discussion with the moral equality of each and every human being. They also show students engaging with addressing the inequality of how, navigating across vast political, social and generational differences and deliberating both about what amounts of education to distribute, given very different experiences, and the content of that education. All four address how different educational moments—listening, memorializing, reflecting or connecting—might offer opportunities to engage with the inequalities of whom. All, as processes of learning linked with research, attempt to use conceptual framings, data and critical reflection to navigate some of the inequalities of how, listening across generations, different experiences of genocides or dispossession. The pedagogy entailed in my work with the students entailed a very alert attention to this inequality of how, much easier to realize through the in depth work of the dissertation, and not full accomplished in the work of the student whose thinking was confined to a 5000 word essay. The vignettes are presented to show how pedagogies matter, and require constant critical reflection on why some kinds of engagements with global injustice are more fully realized as moments of democratic iteration, and others appear to close off insight.

Conclusion

This article has reflected on different forms of inequality and some of the pedagogic relationships entailed in thinking about global inequalities and injustice. The discussion has considered how deploying ideas about different kinds of inequalities and different kinds of obligations, drawing on frameworks from cosmopolitanism and the capability approach, can enhance processes of democratic iteration and help to deepen understandings of these processes for learners and teachers grappling with aspects of global injustice and conditions of plurality, connection and uncertainty. Reflecting on some of my own work, and those who have studied with me, the analysis highlights the considerable resources needed of time, space, social networks, theoretical and empirical engagement and complex understandings of the relationships of the middle, that work across top-down and bottom-up settings. For many teachers working in schools, universities and colleges of education under conditions of pressure and constrained resource, in-depth pedagogic encounters of this sort may indeed be difficult to achieve or sustain. Nonetheless, public education and the pedagogic relationships within it remains an iterative space of possibility. More than three million people around the world voted in the on line poll regarding the world we want post-2015.

TEACHERS MATTER – BUT HOW?

The largest vote across all age groups, men and women, and all regions was for a good education. If the world we want is an educated world, teachers matter crucially. The pedagogic relationships they can develop will help us articulate our visions of global justice, sustainability and equity and allow us to look critically at different kinds of inequality and forms of belonging. Thus, central to some of the concerns with addressing global injustice are engagements with teachers' agency. This requires support for our capacities as teachers to understand and address different kinds of inequalities. It entails all of us engaged with education continuing to reflect on how we draw on skills of negotiating the general and the particular to take forward concerns with equity. Teachers matter, and the matter of teaching can help us engage with global injustice and inequality. Attempting to understand marks a beginning of attempting to bring about change.

Disclosure statement

No potential conflict of interest was reported by the author.

References

Alexander, R. (2008). *Essays on pedagogy*. Abingdon: Routledge.

Andreotti, V. O. (2015). Global citizenship education otherwise. In A. Abdi (Ed.), *Decolonizing global citizenship education* (pp. 221–228). Sense Publishers: Rotterdam.

Andrews, K. (2013). *Fragmented memories: Women, experience and place in Rwanda's genocide memorialisation* (Unpublished MA dissertation). London: Institute of Education, University of London.

Anthias, F. (2008). Thinking through the lens of translocational positionality: An intersectionality frame for understanding identity and belonging. *Translocations: Migration and Social Change, 4*, 5–20.

Anthias, F., & Yuval-Davis, N. (1993). *Racialized boundaries: Race, nation, gender, colour and class and the anti-racist struggle*. London: Routledge.

Auld, E., & Morris, P. (2014). Comparative education, the 'New Paradigm' and policy borrowing: Constructing knowledge for educational reform. *Comparative Education, 50*, 129–155.

Benhabib, S. (1995). Cultural complexity, moral interdependence, and the global dialogical. In M. Nussbaum and J. Glover. (Eds.), *Women, culture, and development: A study of human capabilities* (pp. 235–258). Oxford: Oxford Univeristy Press.

Benhabib, S. (2006). *Another cosmopolitanism*. Oxford: Oxford University Press.

Benhabib, S. (2011). *Dignity in adversity: Human rights in troubled times*. Cambridge: Polity.

Brock, G. (Ed.). (2013a). *Cosmopolitanism versus non-cosmopolitanism: Critiques, defenses, reconceptualizations*. Oxford: Oxford University Press.

Brock, G. (2013b). Rethinking the cosmopolitanism versus non-cosmopolitanism debate: An introduction. In G. Brock. (Ed.), *Cosmopolitanism versus non-cosmopolitanism: Critiques, defenses, reconceptualizations*. (pp. 1–31). Oxford: Oxford University Press.

Butler, J. (2010). *Frames of war*. London: Verso.

Education and International Development. (2013, November). *Mission statement of the education and international development section*. Statement adopted by staff of the Education and International Development Section, Department of Humanities and Social Science, Institute of Education, University of London, London.

Garrison, J. (1997). *Wisdom and desire in the art of teaching*. New York, NY: Teachers' College Press.

Hansen, D. (2011). *The teacher and the world: A study of cosmopolitanism as education. Teacher quality and school development*. Abingdon: Routledge, Taylor & Francis.

Harvey, D. (2013). *Cosmopolitanism and the geographies of freedom*. New York, NY: Columbia University Press.

Hayden, M. J. (2013). Arendt and cosmopolitanism: The human conditions of cosmopolitan teacher education. *Ethics & Global Politics, 5*, 239–258.

Ignatieff, M. (2014). The new world disorder. *The New York Review of Books, LX!*, 14, 25 September.

Klees, S. J., & Qargha, O. (2014). Equity in education: The case of UNICEF and the need for participative debate. *Prospects, 44*, 321–333.

Marshall, H. (2009). Educating the European citizen in the global age: Engaging with the post-national and identifying a research agenda. *Journal of Curriculum Studies, 41*, 247–267.

Mason, P. (2016). *Postcapitalism: A guide to our future*. London: Macmillan.

Moellendorf, D. (2013). Human dignity, associative duties, and egalitarian global justice. In G. Brock (Ed.), *Cosmopolitanism versus non-cosmopolitanism: Critiques, defenses, reconceptualizations* (pp. 222–237). Oxford: Oxford University Press.

Moore, A. (2012). *Teaching and learning: Pedagogy, curriculum and culture*. Abingdon: Routledge.

Morris, P. (2015). Comparative education, PISA, politics and educational reform: A cautionary note. *Compare: A Journal of Comparative and International Education, 45*, 470–474.

Nussbaum, M. (2011). *Creating capabilities*. Cambridge, MA: Harvard University Press.

Omaar, L. (2015). *Investigating the dynamics of displacement among Somali female refugee students in Eastleigh, Nairobi* (Unpublished dissertation prepared for MA in Education), Gender and International Development, Institute of Education, University College London, London.

Parkes, J. (Ed.). (2015). *Gender violence in poverty contexts: The educational challenge*. Abingdon: Routledge.

Piketty, T. (2016). *Chronicles on our troubled time*. London: Viking.

Popkewitz, T. S. (2012). *Cosmopolitanism and the age of school reform: Science, education, and making society by making the child*. New York, NY: Routledge.

Rovisco, M., & Nowicka, M. (Eds.). (2013). *The Ashgate research companion to cosmopolitanism*. Farnham: Ashgate.

Sahlberg, P. (2011). *Finnish lessons*. New York, NY: Teachers College Press.

Schiller, N. G., & Irving, A. (Eds.). (2014). *Whose cosmopolitanism?: Critical perspectives, relationalities and discontents*. Oxford: Berghahn Books.

Sen, A. (1980). Equality of what?, In S. M. MacMurrin (Ed.), *The tanner lectures on human values* (2nd ed, 2010, pp. 195–220). Cambridge: Cambridge University Press.

Sen, A. (1992). *Inequality reexamined*. Oxford: Clarendon Press.

Sen, A. (1999). *Development as freedom*. Oxford: Oxford University Press.

Starkey, H. (2012). Human rights, cosmopolitanism and utopias: Implications for citizenship education. *Cambridge Journal of Education, 42*, 21–35.

Stewart, F. (2000). Crisis prevention: Tackling horizontal inequalities. *Oxford Development Studies, 28*, 245–262.

Stewart, F. (2009). Horizontal inequality: Two types of trap. *Journal of Human Development and Capabilities, 10*, 315–340.

Tokuda, M. (2005). *Somebody is listening: Making and remaking of memories of Okinawan women* (Unpublished MA dissertation). London: Institute of Education, University of London.

Unterhalter, E. (2009). What is equity in education? Reflections from the capability approach. *Studies in Philosophy and Education, 28*, 415–424.

Unterhalter, E. (2012). Inequality, capabilities and poverty in four African countries: Girls' voice, schooling, and strategies for institutional change. *Cambridge Journal of Education, 42*, 307–325.

Unterhalter, E. (2015a). Analysing inequalities in education. In T. McCowan & E. Unterhalter (Eds.), *Education and international development: An introduction* (pp. 127–148). London: Bloomsbury.

Unterhalter, E. (2015b). *Measuring gender inequality and equality in education*. Concept paper prepared for United Nations Girls' Education Initiative workshop, London, September. Retrieved April 2016, from https://en.unesco.org/gem-report/sites/gem-report/files/Workshop%20Concept%20PaperI.pdf

Unterhalter, E. (2016). *Teacher education, teacher practice, gender and girls' schooling outcomes* (A study in five Nigerian states. Executive summary of research report). Abuja: British Council.

Valentini, L. (2013). Cosmopolitan justice and rightful enforceability. In G. Brock (Ed.), *Cosmopolitanism versus non-cosmopolitanism: Critiques, defenses, reconceptualizations* (pp. 92–107). Oxford: Oxford University Press.

Young, I. M. (2011). *Responsibility for justice*. Oxford: Oxford University Press.

Young, M. (2012). Education, globalization and the 'Voice of Knowledge'. In D. Livingstone & D. Guile (Eds.), *The knowledge economy and lifelong learning* (pp. 335–347). Rotterdam: Sense Publishers.

Young, M. (2013). Overcoming the crisis in curriculum theory: A knowledge-based approach. *Journal of Curriculum Studies, 45*, 101–118.

Yuval-Davis, N. (2011). *The politics of belonging: Intersectional contestations*. London: Sage.

Yuval-Davis, N., & Anthias, F. (Eds.). (1989). *Woman, nation, state*. London: Macmillan.

Zeng, M. (2014). Subaltern cosmopolitanism: concept and approaches. *The Sociological Review, 62*, 137–148.

∂ OPEN ACCESS

Talking about education: exploring the significance of teachers' talk for teacher agency

Gert Biesta ⓘ, Mark Priestley and Sarah Robinson

ABSTRACT
The interest in teachers' discourses and vocabularies has for a long time been studied under the rubric of knowledge, most notably teachers' professional knowledge. This interest can be traced back to Shulman's distinction between different kinds of teacher knowledge and Schwab's interest in the role of practical reasoning and judgement in teaching. Within the research, a distinction can be found between a more narrow approach that focuses on teachers' propositional or theoretical knowledge and a more encompassing approach in which teachers' knowledge is not only the knowledge *for* teachers generated elsewhere, but also the knowledge *of* teachers. This is the 'stock of knowledge' gained from a range of sources and experiences, including teachers' ongoing engagement with the practice of teaching itself. In this paper, we focus on the role of teachers' talk in their achievement of agency. We explore how, in what way and to what extent such talk helps or hinders teachers in exerting control over and giving direction to their everyday practices, bearing in mind that such practices are not just the outcome of teachers' judgements and actions, but are also shaped by the structures and cultures within which teachers work.

Introduction: teacher agency and teacher talk

The interest in teachers' discourses and vocabularies has for a long time been studied under the rubric of knowledge, most notably teachers' professional knowledge. This interest can be traced back to Shulman's distinction between different kinds of teacher knowledge—content knowledge, general knowledge, curriculum knowledge, pedagogical content knowledge, knowledge of learners and their characteristic, knowledge of educational contexts, knowledge of educational ends, purposes, and values and their philosophical and historical grounds (see Shulman, 1986, p.8)—and Schwab's interest in the role of practical reasoning and judgement in teaching (see Biesta, 2013; Schwab, [1970] 2013). This work is itself embedded within wider discourses about knowledge and judgement in a broad range of professional practices (see, e.g. Eraut, 1994; Schön, 1983, 1987).

This is an Open Access article distributed under the terms of the Creative Commons Attribution License (http://creativecommons.org/licenses/by/4.0/), which permits unrestricted use, distribution, and reproduction in any medium, provided the original work is properly cited.

Within the research on teacher knowledge a distinction can be found between a more 'narrow' approach that focuses on teachers' propositional or theoretical knowledge—nowadays often connected to scientifically validated evidence about 'what works' (see Biesta, 2007 for an overview and critical discussion)—and a more 'encompassing' approach in which teachers' knowledge is not only the knowledge *for* teachers generated elsewhere, but also the knowledge *of* teachers (for the distinction see Fenstermacher, 1994). This is the 'stock of knowledge' gained from a range of sources and experiences, including teachers' ongoing engagement with the practice of teaching itself (see, e.g. Ben-Peretz, 2011). Whereas some research has tried to move away from the personal and the experiential towards the construction of a common or shared 'knowledge base' for teaching (e.g. Verloop, Van Driel, & Meijer, 2001), other research has explicitly stayed with teachers' 'personal practical knowledge' (Connelly & Clandinin, 1988) in order to deepen understanding of the complexities and significance of such embodied practical knowledge. This work has taken a particular interest in the narrative dimensions of such knowledge (see Connelly & Clandinin, 1988, see also Goodson, Biesta, Tedder, & Adair, 2010).

Our interest in this paper is on the role of teachers' talk in their achievement of agency. We are interested, in other words, in how, in what way and to what extent such talk helps or hinders teachers in exerting control over and giving direction to their everyday practices, bearing in mind that such practices are not just the outcome of teachers' judgements and actions, but are also shaped by the structured and cultures within which teachers work. The paper builds on our research into the conditions that shape and support teacher agency (see Biesta, Priestley, & Robinson, 2015; Priestley, Biesta, Philippou, & Robinson, 2015; Priestley, Biesta, & Robinson, 2015a, 2015b). The particular context in which we raised these questions was the implementation of *Curriculum for Excellence*, a reform of the Scottish education system for children and young people aged 3 to 18 that explicitly sought to enhance the agency of teachers in the development and enactment of curriculum (see Priestley & Biesta, 2013). *Curriculum for Excellence* was developed during the first decade of the twenty-first century, and implementation started from the 2010 to 2011 school year onwards (see http://educationscotland.gov.uk).

We conducted small-scale ethnographic research within a single education authority in Scotland, in one primary school and two secondary schools. Participants comprised two experienced classroom teachers plus a single senior line manager in each school, all of whom were interviewed at least once, and in most cases three or more times. Data were generated over three distinct phases, following an iterative design where each phase was partially determined by the findings of the previous phase. Data collection involved observation; semi-structured individual and group interviews, including, at the start of the project, a personal and professional history interview; analysis of key policy texts; and teacher network mapping. Project researchers spent several weeks in total in each setting, for example, conducting interviews and leading group sessions. Project data were analysed using a set of codes derived from the teacher agency model discussed in the next section, which allowed us to categorize findings according to the key concepts surrounding agency.

Teacher agency and teachers' talk: an ecological approach

Against the tendency to think of agency as a capacity or ability individuals possess, we have pursued an *ecological* understanding of agency that focuses on the question how agency is *achieved* in concrete settings and under particular ecological conditions and circumstances (Biesta & Tedder, 2006). This ecological view of agency sees agency as an emergent phenomenon of the ecological conditions through which it is enacted, highlighting

> that actors always *act by means* of their environment rather than simply in their environment [so that] the achievement of agency will always result from the interplay of individual efforts, available resources and contextual and structural factors as they come together in particular and, in a sense, always unique situations. (Biesta & Tedder, 2007, p. 137)

Agency is therefore both a temporal and a relational phenomenon; it is something that occurs over time and is about the relations between actors and the environments in and through which they act.

In our understanding of agency we draw on Emirbayer and Mische (1998), who have sought to theorise agency in such a way as to overcome the theoretical one-sidedness of existing theories. Such theories tend to focus either on *routine*—that is, on the experience and expertise teachers bring to their work—or on *purpose*—that is on the orientations that guide teachers' work—or on *judgement*—that is, on the decisions teachers make about what to do and how to do it in the here and now. Emirbayer and Mische make a case for a theory of agency that encompasses the dynamic interplay between these three dimensions and which takes into consideration 'how this interplay varies within different structural contexts of action' (Emirbayer & Mische, 1998, p. 963). For this reason, they suggest that the achievement of agency should be understood as a configuration of influences from the *past*, orientations towards the *future* and engagement with the *present*. They refer to these three dimensions as the *iterational*, the *projective* and the *practical-evaluative* dimension, respectively.[1]

Taking an ecological approach to teacher agency and acknowledging that in the achievement of agency past, future and present all play a role, begins to suggest that there are quite a lot things that may affect—positively or negatively—the ways in which and the extent to which teachers achieve agency in the always concrete and unique settings in which they work. In other publications we have explored the role of values and beliefs (Biesta et al., 2015), the impact of cultures of performativity (Priestley, Robinson, & Biesta, 2012) and the intersections between teacher agency and curriculum policy and practice (Priestley, Biesta, & Robinson, 2013). What cuts across many of these discussions is the role played by the vocabularies teachers deploy—or in more mundane terms: teachers talk—not only because such vocabularies allow teachers to make sense of the situations they are in, but also because they shape their expectations and ambitions, their views about what is possible and what not, both with regard to themselves and their actions, and with regard to the colleagues they work with and the students they work for. We thus see teachers' talk as an important *resource* for the achievement of agency. In what follows we seek to make visible what this resource looks like, and also where it comes from and how it functions in teachers' speaking, thinking and doing. The data we discuss are from repeated semi-structured interviews with teachers and head teachers/senior managers in primary and secondary schools in Scotland. We use pseudonyms and description of role to identify the participants below.

While we will focus on individual teachers, their talk and the vocabularies that are deployed in their talk, it is of course important to bear in mind that such vocabularies are not invented by teachers but are the outcome of the complex interaction between personal sense-making and wider discourses that emanate from a range of different sources, including policy, research and public opinion (see, e.g. Nichols & Griffith, 2009). As we will show in this contribution, some of these discourses are powerful because they are part of the official structures and cultures within teachers work, such as, for example, discourses about (measurable) student achievement. Other discourses are powerful because they are fashionable within educational circles, such as, for example, the 'new language of learning' (Biesta, 2006), where pupils and students have been redefined as learners, teaching has become the facilitation of learning and schools have been redesignated as learning environments and places for learning. The language of learning has been quickly co-opted in many educational circles and has put pressure on an older and in a sense more explicitly normative language of education, one in which the point of schooling is not defined in terms of facilitating students' learning, but where there is a clear engagement with the question of purpose, that is the question what the learning is supposed to be *for* (Biesta, 2015).

In the sections that follow, we intend to show how the ways teachers talk figures in their thinking and doing and how this reflects on their sense of agency. We do this through a thematic presentation of insights from the data analysis which will also allow us to show how the ways teachers talk 'in' and 'about' education is connected to their personal and professional experience and the wider discourses that have informed and shaped their personal and professional biography. This will also allow us to make visible how some of such discourses seem to support the ways in which teachers make sense of their practice, while others seem to interfere with and distort what they feel matters and should matter in education. In the concluding section, we summarize what we think that the exploration of teachers talk tells us about its role and significance for teachers' sense of agency and their potential achievement of agency.

Talking about education: Rachael

One crucial question in relation to the theme of this paper is what teachers actually talk about when they talk about education. How, in other words, do they see the 'project' of education and what do they think that the particular task of the school is? Not surprisingly, some teachers have a more articulate way to talk about this than others. Rachael, one of the primary teachers in our project, in response to our question about what education is for, said that it was 'for growing and living, for life'.

> If we didn't have learning then you wouldn't be able to have the skills in order to survive in anything that starts from the basic skills you learn just as a baby. (…) Gradually growing up. And then it is obviously more advanced skills. [Rachael]

She did not think, though, that children would perceive it in this way as well.

> (P)eople would not think it is education although, because learning is education. Children, I do not think would see the link. If they were doing something they would not think that they are necessarily having education. They think of education as anything that happened in school, like written things. [Rachael]

For Rachael there is, therefore, on the one hand a clear distinction between learning as something that can happen all the time and everywhere—'There is never a point when there is not learning happening'—and what the school is for, although it is interesting that in her way of talking, 'learning' is also what is key in the school. In response to the question what school is for, she said:

> Well, the main thing you would come straight away is for learning. But not just academic learning. You are building them as individuals to know how to relate to others, how to socialise, interact. To get them prepared for the wider world. [Rachael]

This wider world is particularly conceived in terms of the world of work, which, for Rachael, is an important element of the life for which schools should prepare children.

> And I probably just link it to [work] because you see life as well if you do not work then you are not going to be living much of a life cause you are not going to be making any money. So a lot of it is linked to work. [Rachael]

What is interesting in relation to the particular context of our research is that Rachael appears to have adopted the idea that *Curriculum for Excellence* marks a shift in thinking and doing from a focus on knowledge to a focus on skills. She not only sees a strong distinction between education focused on knowledge and education focused on life, but is also quite negative about the former, thus echoing a rather common [mis]perception that skills do not require knowledge or that having knowledge or being knowledgeable is devoid of any skills (on this see Gill & Thomson, 2012).

> Is it nice to learn things, facts, but that cannot be transferred. That is not going to help them when they leave school. (…) Whereas the skills that help them learn those things or do a certain activity in a certain way is what will help them in the future. [Rachael]

During the 6 years that she has been a teacher, she does see this as an important shift in her thinking and in her practice.

> I supposed I have gradually changed in that way that, well I suppose because it is quite all about knowledge. You are not really thinking as much about the skills. (…) Cause you are busy wanting your end product from them. But really the process should take a lot longer 'cause you should be teaching them the elements to put all together to make this final. So yeah, I do think it has changed. [Rachael]

Talking about education: Eilidh

The emphasis *Curriculum for Excellence* places on skills is also what Eilidh, another primary teacher we spoke with, mentioned as a key aspect of how it has 'landed' in her school. This partly has to do with the discourse of *Curriculum for Excellence* itself, though Eilidh also mentioned that in her school they had decided 'on about twelve skills we felt as a school, that if we can do these, then our children will leave [our school] as better people'.

Whereas, Rachael not only perceived *Curriculum for Excellence* in terms of a shift from knowledge to skills but also saw this as a desirable shift, Eilidh saw this far less as an opposition. In her view, 'as an educator you do need to teach the knowledge as well as the skills'. More generally, her talk was more detailed and perhaps we could also say that it was more nuanced—something that may have to do with the fact that she had been in education for a much longer period of time than Rachael (see the next section). Here is, for example, how she spoke about her task of being a teacher.

> I think … if I look at it I think it changes between primary one and primary seven. I think in primary one initially it is very much a nurturing and the rules of behaviour within a school have to … you have to pull them back in some ways. It can't be free. An awful lot of them live outside, in their own society where they do what they want, when they want, how they want. And it is just to try and get them back into the fact that, 'no that is not it, we have our rules in here and you have to become a valued member of this school', but in order to do that there has to be respect shown and given.

> So whereas by primary seven hopefully a lot of that has been instilled, but you have got the few, and it is a few, who are pulling against society even at ten, eleven years old. Fighting against it. It is them, it is a control thing and bringing them back and trying to … But as an educator you do need to teach the knowledge as well as the skills. So as much as it is about teaching the skills so they can go out, there has to be certain amounts of knowledge. It is clichés, the

relevance of it all. But I think if you do show them that, if you couldn't read, you can't go into the bus station and read the times of the trains, how are you going to find the times of the trains? You can't use your computer. It is about trying to show them that 'yes you might find it boring when I am doing this all about timetables, but actually here is the reason for it'. And I think we are beginning to do that a lot more. [Eilidh]

Whereas both Rachael and Eilidh connect the 'point' of education with future participation in society, including the world of work, Eilidh's account appears to have more detail. The fact that balance is important in her account is also reflected in the way in which she compared her own experiences at school with the current situation.

The only thing that I can remember from school, and it is such a long time ago from primary, would be the very definite mornings for maths and language work, and the afternoons for the fun activities. I think that what we have got now is far better. I think we integrate much more and the children who maybe won't succeed at the maths and language side of it will succeed in many other areas of the curriculum. I personally wasn't classed as a bright pupil because my English skills were not wonderful in primary. But we didn't do the gym, which I excelled in. We didn't do a lot of arty type things. But it was all very much on writing, reading and initially, once I moved up obviously ... but secondary school, I just remember it being extremely academic based. Sit down, get on with it, and if you could then you succeeded and if you didn't you went into some other form of employment. I suppose even in my day, moving out to another form of employment was still possible whereas nowadays it is much more difficult. [Eilidh]

Age and generation: Rachael and Eilidh

While it is difficult to pin down why the two ways in which these teachers talk differ, one important aspect seems to have to do with the fact that stems from different professional generations. Rachael had only been teaching for 6 years whereas Eilidh had been 'in the system' for nearly 30 years already—referring to herself as a 'crabbit old teacher'. There are two aspects that need to be taken into consideration here; one which we might call an *age-effect*—that is, the impact of having been around for a longer period of time—and the other a *generation-effect*, where Eilidh, in her own teacher education and in earlier stages of her career, may have been exposed to very different views about education and very different education practices.

The 'age-effect' is clearly visible in the following remark where Eilidh emphasizes that older ideas seem to be coming back.

I have seen, in teaching, the child centred, the integrated day, the whole class teaching, five to fourteen and then back round to this more child centred, integration on everything again. They always do say that you come round in circles. And that is where I am now, thinking actually what I am doing now in primary one, because I started off in a primary one, a lot of similarities. [Eilidh]

Yet she is also aware that she has become more experienced and more confident over time.

I think I have become better. I think ... when I think back to some of the lessons I maybe did when I first started and I think 'oh gosh, I didn't do that did I?' and I know we all learn by mistakes and sometimes it is no bad thing because then you can talk about it and discuss it, even with the children. But I think because you have made these mistakes you become a better teacher. I go to do something and then I don't have to think too much about it, because I think 'that is not going to work, change it'. Whereas maybe twenty years ago, I would have tried it and it didn't work, so the next time I have not. [Eilidh]

Taking the impact of age/experience and generation together we can see that Eilidh has access to a discourse that gives her a 'bigger picture' and that allows her to put things in perspective. In this regard, we can say that Rachael seems to be more dependent on the policy discourse of *Curriculum for Excellence*, at least partly because she had not yet had the opportunity to experience and work through a series of policy- and practice-shifts and thus has had less opportunity to develop her discursive 'resources'. What is clear from the discussion above is that such resources—more concretely, the way teachers talk about and understand education, the school and their role as a teacher—provide an important window on the situation they are in; a reflective window both to perceive and to evaluate what is going on and what is absent or missing.

The personal and the professional: Shona

Such discourses are, however, not just personal/biographical but are also related to the particular responsibilities one has as a teacher. They are, in other words, also a function of the particular ecological conditions of teachers' work. This is clearly visible in some of the ways in which Shona, headteacher of the primary school in our project, spoke about her work, the school and education more generally. On the one hand, her talk is obviously influenced by the particular set of responsibilities that come with the role, and thus they reflect some of the outside expectations and pressures quite well. This is first of all visible in how she sees her role within the school.

> So I am responsible for absolutely everything. I am responsible for health and safety. I am responsible for the educational development of the pupils. I am responsible for all the legislative requirements that they have to implement to make sure that health and safety is in place. Additional support needs legislation is being followed. All the child protection stuff, assessments, risk assessments, educational excursions assessments, the whole quality assurance agenda, the provision of the curriculum, parental complaints, personnel issues, everything. [Shona]

Yet there is another side to her talk, which is visible in her views about good education where, as she put it, 'really just all hinges in terms of the catchment area'.

> It is a very mixed catchment area. (…) I totally believe in the principles [in a policy document], which is about trying to break the cycle of deprivation within [the local authority]. And to ensure that pupils have the opportunity to maximise their potential. And to give them as much of a holistic approach, experience as possible so that they have the opportunity to experience success and to motivate and galvanise. And just break this whole cycle of deprivation. That is what I believe. [Shona]

While attainment matters in relation to such wider views about the point and purpose of education, it is clear that attainment is not an aim in itself, but in her view of education it serves a wider purpose. There is, in other words, a different 'story' about education that has a strong motivating force. Interestingly, in this case it is connected to this teacher's own educational biography. When asked whether she believes that the school can indeed break the cycle of deprivation, she responded in the following way.

> Well I came myself from an area that is considered to be a deprived area in [name of town]. I came from [name of area]. And my mother was a home help. My father was an electrician. They were very hardworking people. And I suppose I was quite fortunate in as much as I was an only child. So I never actually lacked anything. But the driving force for me was always that they had high values about education. Education was always seen as the way of getting a good job. 'And if you stick in at school you will get a good job'. And I always wanted to please and I wanted to make them proud of me so I worked hard. But I wanted this good job because I wanted to have a nice house and I wanted to have nice holidays. And this had all been indoctrinated in a way. 'You need to do this. You need to get a good job. You do not want to be working as a home help or doing what I have had to do, working in a factory. You need to work hard'. [Shona]

These biographical experiences provide a strong educational 'story' that clearly impacts on how she looks at the present.

> But if we replay that situation to this context just now, I am not sure that I would have been able to go to University because I would have had to make choices about big debts because they would not have been able to fund me. I know from my own personal experience that it costs a lot of money to educate a child at University. And it can go on for a long time. And I do not know how I would have been able to access that. I do not know enough about the system. I just know that for my daughter we did not get any help and we had to fund it all ourselves. And my mum and dad certainly could not have done that. So I suppose there must be ways round that. But it would mean that you end University having a huge amount of debt. And my mother and father do not like debt. So they might have been pushing me in other directions. More about trying to get a job with the qualifications that you get when you leave school. [Shona]

It is therefore not surprising that she believes 'that education can make a difference—otherwise I do not think I would want to be doing the job that I am doing'. Within her talk there is a strong emphasis on skills and on values—'Good positive values. Our school motto is respect'. While she sees the focus on skills as 'one of the big changes' brought about by *Curriculum for Excellence*, she emphasizes that in her school '(w)e have always taken the trouble to provide opportunities for pupils to develop the kind of skills and attributes required by Curriculum for Excellence', so in this regard she does not think 'it is going to make a huge difference'.

Talking about education: Suzie

The way in which our research was designed—interviewing and observing teachers in different primary and secondary schools—makes it possible to see to what extent the vocabularies teachers utilize in their work are personal/professional and to what extent they are related to the particular ecologies in which they work, that is, the cultures and structures that shape their context for action. While we did notice differences, there are also many similarities when we focus on the ways in which the teachers from secondary schools spoke about education.

The conversations we had with Suzie, a senior manager at one of the secondary schools, provided a very clear example of what above we have termed the generation effect. The comparison between the past and the present was frequently depicted as a loss, thus indicating that things as they are nowadays were not as good as they were in the past.

For example, when talking about the tendency in education to measure and assess everything, she provided the following observation.

> We have lost the capacity to explore. To feel our way because for whatever reason we have become less secure, less happy with that because perhaps other people are less happy with it. But for me real learning is about going into the unknown and feeling your way and seeing what you discover and making sense of it. And finding things that you certainly do not know before you start out with. But to me, too many people are not doing that [laughs]. [Suzie]

She actually saw this development itself as a difference between generations.

> For some people in recent years, education has become much more of a job. Teaching has become much more of a job that needs to be done between your employed hours. There is much less of the Scottish approach to education that I came into education embracing and that I have never really lost sight of. And people of my generation in teaching, most would consider that you are educating the whole person. That you are coming from a position of teacher first, subject teacher second. [Suzie]

Her own teacher education—which she did in the 1970s—played a formative role in her professional formation and, once more, provides a deficiency perspective on present practices.

> Perhaps it says something about our own University education. It certainly does in my case, I know that. That we did not see ourselves first and foremost as having to just deliver our own subject curriculum. We wanted to be part of a family in a school. We wanted to be part of a community and all that goes with that including the negative side of developing a community. And I do not see that in the same numbers as I did when I was a young teacher. [Suzie]

While she welcomed many more recent developments and initiatives, she was concerned about what teachers are doing with them and are able to do with them.

> They are all fantastic initiatives. But no single one of them on their own is enough. They are all part of a teacher's toolkit if you like. But I am worried about that concept of toolkit. It is that that for me has made many staff think along the lines of being a practitioner simply thinking of themselves a jobbing teacher. [Suzie]

For Suzie, teaching is precisely not about the application of a toolkit, but is a craft that needs to be developed and refined through experience—a process that obviously takes time.

There is one further aspect of Suzie's talk that we wish to mention, as it is quite different from what most other teachers spoke about, and is also distinctively different from what policy seems to emphasize, that is, focusing on measurable outcomes. Suzie's talk highlights that education is a difficult process and necessarily has to be difficult.

> The best learning happens after pain. It is about an intellectual pain. It is about recognising that this is not easy. And sometimes you have got to have the conversation that says, 'I am very sorry about this but that is not good enough. What you are doing is just not going to cut the mustard. And we do have to look. I will help you to come to terms with what that is but it is just not up to scratch. This is what needs to be done. Here is where we are. Why are you doing this'. You have to somehow or other encourage somebody to genuinely get to their soul. Without it everything is sitting on the surface. (…) Now my methods of teaching in a classroom have always been to try to encourage young people to come into touch with that soul, if you like. And without it really there is no real learning. (…) But it is painful. [Suzie]

For Suzie, this also has a lot to do with her agency, not least because to challenge and encourage students to stay with what is difficult requires conviction and a degree of courage. There is a clear decision point in relation to this.

> So you decide, do you challenge that and take all the fall out that goes with that? Or do you go over the surface of it and just accept it? There are some people who will accept it. And there are some people who will say, 'my integrity stops me from being able to continue with that'. [Suzie]

She is aware that being principled about what matters in education makes the job less easy—'in a way I give myself a lot of extra grief' is how she described it. And again she sees this more principled stance disappearing—again a loss in comparison to the past.

> But the voice inside me, my educational voice, my experienced voice that tells me I have got to address this, means I take on the difficulty. And stirring up the puddle tends to mean it gets clearer in the end. But I do not know whether we live in a time now where many people are of that same opinion. And that people are looking for an easy life. I hear it here with people, 'how long have I got to go before I am home'. [Suzie]

Policy discourses: Monica and Kate

While Suzie's talk was quite elaborate and specific, other teachers in our research had a way of talking about education that was much closer to the policy discourse of learning and of skills. When asked, for example, what education is for, one of the other teachers responded in a way quite similar to what we have seen from one of the primary teachers.

> It is to learn. To help children to learn. But I wouldn't always agree that you are only learning in school. I think people are learning all the time. (…) I think education is all about learning from each other as well as guiding children to learn new things. (…) I think probably when you come into teaching at first you think you teach a subject and that is it. Then I quickly realised that I am actually having to teach social skills here. I am having to teach children how to learn. How to use skills to help them learn. And I think I was probably quite naive when I came into teaching. I thought they would know to put a title at the top of the page, and the date, and that sort of thing. But it is all these little things as well that you are teaching them. Teaching them how to be organised. Teaching them how to have relationships, to have manners, to think … [Monica]

If this answer to the question what education is *for* stayed quite close to the language of learning and of skills, another teacher in the same school articulated this differently.

> Preparing the pupils for whatever they want to do and giving them choices and opportunities to do things that otherwise they would not do if they were not in education. To try and give them a broader outlook on life and different people and different ways of living and different things that they could do in the future. [Kate]

When asked whether education was about transmitting particular pieces of knowledge so that students can pass exams, Kate was quick to respond with a 'No I do not think so', although she did acknowledge that it is 'what we are measured on', and that it is important for pupils in that 'if they have decided that they want to go a certain route, so say they decide they want to be a doctor, then obviously they do need to pass certain exams so it becomes much more about that'.

Experience outside school: Susan

One further point to mention is that both Monica and Kate had come to teaching later in their life. We mention this because having a career outside of education before becoming a teacher is the exception more than the rule. In this regard, it is interesting that in the group of teachers who took part in the project—who were teachers identified by their managers as being quite agentic—we had three teachers who had not followed the more standard career that takes teachers from school, to a degree, to teacher education and back into school. Perhaps this also explains why their talk about education was more limited and probably more influenced by current and recent policy than was the case with other teachers. This is not meant as a judgement about their vocabularies, but just as an observation. It may well be that, over time, these teachers will expand their professional discourse due to ongoing experience of working in education.

One of the teachers we interviewed in the other secondary school, Susan, also had a career outside of education before she entered the teaching profession. Susan's talk about education is an interesting mix of a more fashionable/contemporary language that sees education as being about 'encouraging the learner', 'personalisation and choice', the teacher as 'a facilitator', 'skills for living, skills for life', and setting students on the road 'to fulfil their potential', and observations and ways of conceiving of education that are quite critical of how some of these ideas play out in *Curriculum for Excellence* and how education more generally seems to have drifted away from what matters to her.

> Education has got less and less to do with the individual pupils. And it values individuality less and less. And it appears to me to have become more bureaucratic and top heavy. And when

there is so little money available for education and the budgets are being cut, they are being cut in the wrong place. It is actually bodies in the classroom that is needed. Not at management and higher levels. And it is encouraging pupils to learn. And the people who encourage the learner are the ordinary teachers, the ones who enjoy doing what they do and inspire. And that is the role of a teacher; it is to inspire them to want to learn more. Not necessarily about the subject you are teaching but just to inspire them to learn anything. [Susan]

While on the one hand Susan saw education as a very individual journey, and whereas she recognized that this is a key idea in *Curriculum for Excellence*, she did not see a significant gap between theory and practice.

Personalisation and choice! That sounds brilliant but in actual fact that is not going to be what it is. It is going to be personalisation of choice of the teacher teaching the subject. Not the pupil. [Susan]

She expressed similar doubts about the idea that students should be responsible for their own learning because she believes that 'they do not actually understand what responsibility for their own learning is, and they are not capable of managing it'. She describes the predicament in relation to this as follows:

And the more able pupils still want classroom teaching from the front. They want to have things written down. They want to be taught in the old established way of teaching. And that is what they want because they see that as their route to get to further education. The less able pupils prefer the less structure, but they are in actual fact the ones who are less able to manage their own learning. Yet that is where the focus is. [Susan]

Also, while she was aware of the influence of testing on the practice of education, she made a clear distinction between what is being tested and what matters for her, although she did encounter situations where she was 'in the minority' as someone 'actually who was teaching broadly, not just to the exam'. 'The reality', as she said, 'is we are judged by the end result of exams'. But this implies that significant achievements that fall outside of the scope of what is being examined are not really acknowledged, which was obviously a source of frustration for her.

I had a brilliant experience with a pupil through four, five, six years of somebody who is not achieving A grades and whatever. But you have seen them grow to be lovely human beings. (…) But that is not valued. That is not measurable in a league table. But the point where they have got to from when they come into you at age eleven or twelve, to the point when they leave at sixteen, seventeen or eighteen. There can be a huge development that is not measurable on an education statistical table. (…) But that is such an important part of growing up. [Susan]

While she felt restricted by the emphasis on exams and measurement, this didn't stop her from achieving what she set out to achieve which, 'on the whole', she believed she could. In this regard one restriction she experienced is time—there is not enough time to do everything she would want to do. Another interesting restriction she mentioned 'is actually the pupils themselves and their attitude to learning in that they can be quite put off learning by previous experience'. She explained her own ability to navigate these complexities in terms of her personality. '(It) is because of who I am. It is because I grab opportunities and run with them'. This is a pattern she didn't always see in other teachers. Some teachers, according to her, 'are not willing to take risks' and the main reason for this lies in 'reliance on exam results and the need to provide evidence—and the evidence of a written piece of work is seen as of more value than something that might be a wall display or powerpoint presentation'. In her view this has affected teachers' confidence: 'Our confidence has been eroded'.

Shaping an educational outlook: Sara

Susan's talk appears to be 'mixed', but it is one that effectively allows her to have a critical perspective on *Curriculum for Excellence,* in that she is able to indicate where the curriculum really matches up with her own views about what matters educationally, and where there are tensions. There are therefore discursive resources that allow her to take a stance towards the prevailing policy—to judge what makes sense and what not. While she does explain her agency predominantly as a personality trait—the kind of person she is—this does not preclude the fact that she has a way to talk about education that not only gives her a drive and sense of direction (the projective dimension) but also allows her to evaluate situations she encounters (the evaluative dimension) and to act on the basis of these evaluations (the practical-evaluative dimension). What is less visible, at least in the data available, is what the origins of her educational discourse were (the iterational dimension).

Shaping an educational outlook: Sara

Sara, one of the other teachers we interviewed in this school provided some more insights into what had shaped her educational outlook, perhaps less so in terms of her educational vocabulary, but definitely in terms of what it means to do a job well, something which she connected to the working class background in which she grew up. Here is how she provided an insight in these experiences.

> My dad was and still is a lorry driver, my mum was a dinner lady and she is now a receptionist. And they were just very much 'you work hard, you do what your teachers tell you.' And that was it. 'I am stuck with my homework', 'right, let's sit down and go over it' and they would help. But they were not pushy. They were there and they supported and encouraged but they never said, 'right, we want you to get five highers and we want you to go to University'. (…) And then when I said, 'I want to go to Uni'. 'Right, fine, okay. We will help you'. Chose my Uni, went to Uni. 'Want to be a teacher'. 'Right, fine'. It was more just 'you work hard, you do as you are told, you give your best'. And because both myself and my brother went down different routes in life and they were always just of the opinion, 'we will support you in whatever way you go'. [Sara]

Not only did this attitude provide her with a set of strong values that gave her own work direction (the projective dimension), it also provided an orientation for her teaching. As for her own perspective, she summarized it as follows:

> You just do a good job. You try your best. You do not muck around. You do not do things you should not do or challenge superiors in a way unless it's obviously something genuine. [Sara]

To which she then added:

> And that is what I try and get across to the kids. You work hard and you do what you are told and you act on the advice you are given. You do not try and cheat or shortcut or squirm your way out of things. If you are struggling, you ask for help. [Sara]

This discourse is actually quite important for her, in that it shapes what she finds important in teaching, both in terms of what she seeks to achieve (the projective dimension) and in terms of how she views and values the situations she encounters (the practical-evaluative dimension).

> As I say, there are some kids in our classes that are looking for a shortcut. And 'can I not drop this, can I not …'. And you are just like 'no. It's a pressure point. You are going to just have to make your peace with that and realise okay for about the next month or two I am going to have to just really really work. But then at the end of that month or two you have got your summer holidays. There is the reward. You get time off and you can do whatever you like'. [Sara]

TEACHERS MATTER – BUT HOW?

That this outlook does provide her with a perspective to judge what she encounters in the present is clear in the following quote.

> But yes there are kids that don't have that mentality. And it is annoying sometimes because it is like the more and more they switch off or detach, the more and more stressed you get. And you think, 'wait a minute, I am not the one doing the exam'. [Sara]

Providing students with structure and a steady 'push' are important in her conception of education, as is also evident in the following passage, where she recounts how, in the longer term, the students are able to see the benefits of this approach. When asked whether she thought she was able to enact these views in the classroom, she said:

> I try to. I really do try. And I think that there are kids that can see I have managed to influence them in a positive way because I try to just say to the kids, 'you know how I always get slagged off for being the organised one and the tidy and all of that'. And I am just like, 'but you have got one whole year's worth of work to wade through for your exam. And the worst thing ever would be if this was like you had a bit of that topic in that folder and a bit of that, and it was all over the shop. So if you start off in an organised way come revision time, everything is there. You are not going to have to have that battle'. And I say to them, 'I know I am the crazy stationery lady. Like how you get crazy cat ladies, I am the crazy stationery lady' [laughs] but there have actually been kids who have said to me, if I had not shown them how to do that, they would have just been an absolute nightmare. But even things as well like when they are doing NABs[2] or their prelims[3] and I am saying to them, 'just because this is not going to the [exam board], do not just opt for your minimum. Show off, do the best that you can'. [Sara]

Here we can see an articulate educational vocabulary, a way of talking and reasoning that gives a strong sense of direction to the practice of this teacher. What is interesting, however, is that there is a clear difference between the places where she feels able to act on the basis of her convictions and ideas and the places where she feels limited in doing so—which again sheds some light on the ecological conditions of the achievement of agency. Where she does feel there is a space for acting on the basis of her ideas is in her own classroom. When we suggested that we felt that she was 'fairly autonomous' in her own classroom, she immediately responded by saying 'oh yes, in my own classroom, absolutely—yes, definitely'.

> And even in the department in terms of [our subject area], yes. And I work with people in my department who think the same way. Like we were talking about [a colleague] last time. So yes it is dead easy there. And on another angle, in the faculty, I am lucky enough to work in a faculty where the leadership has not gone the opposite way and where everything is controlled. [Sara]

So from this angle it looks like she acts in a situation where it is possible to achieve agency, where it is possible to enact a conception of education that clearly matters to her. But this is not all she has to say about it, because when asked about the presence or absence of synergy between her own views and the beliefs and vision of the school, she is more hesitant. The first response to our question here was a 'Mmhmm' and after an 'okay' from us a 'yes' and a laugh.

> There is [sic] different levels of tension. There is one level even within the faculty, I am trying to be very diplomatic here, I will look at certain things and I will think, 'that is really important. That ought to be done properly and it is not being done properly'. And in my head I will think how I would do it. But obviously I am powerless. [Sara]

That in this context she feels that she *is* powerless, indicates that the achievement of agency is not just a matter of capacity or having a clear discourse and a clear sense of direction and of what matters, but is always achieved—or not—in concrete ecological conditions. And whereas at classroom and, to some extent, at faculty level these conditions seem such that it is possible to achieve agency, within the wider context of the school this obviously becomes more challenging.

Discussion and conclusions

In this paper, we have sought to explore the discursive resources that play a role in teachers' achievement of agency. We have tried to characterize the different ways in which the teachers in our project spoke about their practice; we have tried to find out where such talk comes from, including the wider discourses that inform and shape teachers' talk; and we have tried to shed light on the ways in which their talk plays a role in the achievement of agency. A couple of things stand out.

One is that all teachers do have something to say about education, but that some talk is (far) more elaborate and detailed than other and that the different ways in which teachers talk about education reveal different 'strengths' of conviction. In each case, we have seen how the teacher's talk allowed them to have views about the current situation, which has to do with the practical-evaluative dimension of the achievement of agency. In some cases, there was little difference between teachers' talk and the prevailing situation, whereas in other cases there was a significant difference between how the teachers spoke about education and the situations they found themselves in. This at least allowed them to be critical about the current situation, though we have also seen how for some teachers this 'translates' into possibilities for action closer to their own values and convictions. Whether it allows teachers to act differently—and hence to achieve agency—is, however, not only dependent on a critical outlook and a vocabulary that provides an evaluative window on the situation, but remains dependent on the particular ecological conditions under which they act, something that some of the teachers we spoke with in our project were acutely aware of.

Zooming in on teachers talk also made it possible to get a sense of where their talk and their wider vocabularies came from. Here we found a clear biographical dimension, not only in how teachers viewed education but also with regard to their educational values. There was also clear evidence of age-effects—the influence of experience—and generation-effects—the influence of having had experience of very different contexts, practices and ideas, than what currently is prevalent. With some of the teachers this led to a stronger orientation towards the future (the projective dimension of agency) which did appear to make a difference with regard to teachers' actions in the here and how. What was interesting with one of the teachers in the secondary school was that the degree in which she saw herself as being able to achieve agency significantly depended on context—she felt more able within the environment of her own classroom, and felt less able ('powerless') within the wider context of the school.

Finally, we also found clear evidence of the influence of policy discourses—not least the discourse of *Curriculum for Excellence* itself—and wider trends, including many traces of the 'language of learning'.

What our research suggests is that the ways in which teachers talk in and about education is an important resource with regard to their achievement of agency. Teachers' talk, that is, the vocabularies they utilize they when articulate their views about education and their values and visions about what education ought to be, provides an important 'window' on the here and now, that is, on the everyday situations in which teachers act. Here, we can see that the degree to which teachers' vocabularies allow for a perspective *on* those situations plays an important role in their perceived room for manoeuvre, both because it allows for evaluation of the current situation (the evaluative dimension) and for a sense of alternative ways of acting (the projective dimension). Although teachers' talk and the vocabularies they utilize are first of all 'of' the teachers, it is also clear that such talk is not uniquely individual, but is to a degree shared because it emanates from shared histories and because it functions within shared practices. To this comes the fact that teachers' talk is not independent from policy, research and everyday discourses about education, both discourses from the past and discourses from the present.

Perhaps the most striking finding from our research is the degree to which the talk and vocabularies of some teachers appeared to be rather limited and closely connected to policy discourses, hence leading to a situation where there is very little different between teachers' talk and the policy discourses within which they do their work, thus limiting their opportunities for critical evaluation and alternative courses of action. Although teachers' talk is at most a necessary condition for their achievement of agency—our ecological approach highlights that the achievement of agency emanates from the complex interplay of individual capacity and collective cultures and structures—the experiences of the teachers in our project did indicate that such talk can make a crucial difference for teachers' agency. This, in turn, suggests that enhancing the discursive resources of teachers—through initial teacher education and ongoing professional development—remains an important avenue towards a more agentic teacher profession.

Notes

1. In concrete actions all three dimensions play a role, but the degree to which they contribute varies. This is why Emirbayer and Mische speak of a *chordal triad* of agency within which all three dimensions resonate as separate but not always harmonious tones' (Emirbayer & Mische, 1998, p. 972; emphasis in original). In line with this, they propose the following definition of agency as 'the temporally constructed engagement by actors of different structural environments—the temporal-relational contexts of action—which, through the interplay of habit, imagination, and judgement, both reproduces and transforms those structures in interactive response to the problems posed by changing historical situations' (Emirbayer & Mische, 1998, p. 970; emphasis in original). Agency, in other words, thus appears as a 'temporally embedded process of social engagement, informed by the past (in its habitual aspect), oriented towards the future (as a capacity to imagine alternative possibilities) and "acted out" in the present (as a capacity to contextualize past habits and future projects with the contingencies of the moment)' (Emirbayer & Mische, 1998, p. 963).
2. National Assessment Bank tests, used for Higher courses to assess mastery of course content.
3. Preliminary examinations—a dress rehearsal for the real exam to be taken later in the year.

Disclosure statement

No potential conflict of interest was reported by the authors.

Funding

This work was supported by the UK Economic and Social Research Council [grant reference RES-000-22-4208].

ORCID

Gert Biesta http://orcid.org/0000-0001-8530-7105

References

Ben-Peretz, M. (2011). Teacher knowledge. What is it? How do we uncover it? What are its implications for schooling? *Teaching and Teacher Education, 27*, 3–9.

Biesta, G. J. J. (2006). *Beyond learning: Democratic education for a human future*. London: Paradigm Publishers.

Biesta, G. J. J. (2007). Why 'what works' won't work. Evidence-based practice and the democratic deficit of educational research. *Educational Theory, 57*, 1–22.

Biesta, G. J. J. (2013). Knowledge, judgement and the curriculum: On the past, present and future of the idea of the practical. *Journal of Curriculum Studies, 45*, 684–696.

Biesta, G. J. J. (2015). What is education for? On good education, teacher judgement, and educational professionalism. *European Journal of Education, 50*, 75–87.

Biesta, G. J. J., Priestley, M., & Robinson, S. (2015). The role of beliefs in teacher agency. *Teachers and Teaching: Theory and Practice, 21*, 624–640. http://dx.doi.org/10.1080/13540602.2015.1044325.

TEACHERS MATTER – BUT HOW?

Biesta, G. J. J., & Tedder, M. (2006). *How is agency possible? Towards an ecological understanding of agency-as-achievement* (Working Paper 5). Exeter: The Learning Lives project.

Biesta, G. J. J., & Tedder, M. (2007). Agency and learning in the lifecourse: Towards an ecological perspective. *Studies in the Education of Adults, 39*, 132–149.

Connelly, F. M., & Clandinin, D. J. (1988). *Teachers as curriculum planners: Narratives of experience.* New York, NY: Teachers College Press.

Emirbayer, M., & Mische, A. (1998). What is agency? *The American Journal of Sociology, 103*, 962–1023.

Eraut, M. (1994). *Developing professional practice and competence.* London: Falmer Press.

Fenstermacher, G. (1994). The knower and the known: the nature of knowledge in research on teaching. In L. Darling-Hammond (Ed.), *Review of research in education* (Vol. 20, pp. 3–56). Washington, DC: AERA.

Gill, S., & Thomson, G. (2012). *Rethinking secondary education: A human-centred approach.* Harlow: Pearson.

Goodson, I., Biesta, G. J. J., Tedder, M., & Adair, N. (2010). *Narrative learning.* London: Routledge.

Nichols, N., & Griffith, A. I. (2009). Talk, texts, and educational action: An institutional ethnography of policy in practice. *Cambridge Journal of Education, 39*, 241–255.

Priestley, M., & Biesta, G. J. J. (Eds.). (2013). *Reinventing the curriculum. New trends in curriculum policy and practice.* London: Bloomsbury.

Priestley, M., Biesta, G. J. J., Philippou, S., & Robinson, S. (2015). The teacher and the curriculum: Exploring teacher agency. In D. Wyse, L. Hayward, & J. Pandya (Eds.), *The Sage handbook of curriculum, pedagogy and assessment* (pp. 78–91). London: Sage.

Priestley, M., Biesta, G. J. J., & Robinson, S. (2013). Teachers as agents of change: Teacher agency and emerging models of curriculum. In M. Priestley & G. J. J. Biesta (Eds.), *Reinventing the curriculum. New trends in curriculum policy and practice* (pp. 186–206). London: Bloomsbury.

Priestley, M., Biesta, G. J. J., & Robinson, S. (2015a). *Teacher agency: An ecological approach.* London: Bloomsbury.

Priestley, M., Biesta, G. J. J., & Robinson, S. (2015b). Teacher agency: What is it and why does it matter? In R. Kneyber & J. Evers (Eds.), *Flip the system: Changing education from the bottom up* (pp. 134–148). London: Routledge.

Priestley, M., Robinson, S., & Biesta, G. J. J. (2012). Teacher agency, performativity and curriculum change: Reinventing the teacher in the Scottish curriculum for excellence? In B. Jeffrey & G. Troman (Eds.), *Performativity in UK education: Ethnographic cases of its effects, agency and reconstructions* (pp. 87–108). Painswick: E&E Publishing.

Schön, D. A. (1983). *The reflective practitioner: How professionals think in action.* New York, NY: Basic Books.

Schön, D. A. (1987). *Educating the Reflective Practitioner.* San Francisco, CA: Jossey-Bass.

Schwab, J. ([1970] 2013). The practical: A language for curriculum. *Journal of Curriculum Studies, 45*, 591–621.

Shulman, L. S. (1986). Those who understand: Knowledge growth in teaching. *Educational Researcher, 15*, 4–14.

Verloop, N., Van Driel, J., & Meijer, P. (2001). Teacher knowledge and the knowledge base of teaching. *International Journal of Educational Research, 35*, 441–461.

ᵃ OPEN ACCESS

Curriculum policy reform in an era of technical accountability: 'fixing' curriculum, teachers and students in English schools

Christine Winter

ABSTRACT

Drawing on a Levinasian ethical perspective, the argument driving this paper is that the technical accountability movement currently dominating the educational system in England is less than adequate because it overlooks educators' responsibility for ethical relations in responding to difference in respect of the other. Curriculum policy makes a significant contribution to the technical accountability culture through complicity in performativity, high-stakes testing and datafication, at the same time as constituting student and teacher subjectivities. I present two different conceptualizations of subjectivity and education, before engaging these in the analysis of data arising from an empirical study which investigated teachers' and stakeholders' experiences of curriculum policy reform in 'disadvantaged' English schools. The study's findings demonstrate how a prescribed programme of technical curriculum regulation attempts to 'fix' or mend educational problems by 'fixing' or prescribing educational solutions. This not only denies ethical professional relations between students, teachers and parents, but also deflects responsibility for educational success from government to teachers and hastens the move from public to private educational provision. Complying with prescribed curriculum policy requirements shifts attention from broad philosophical and ethical questions about educational purpose as well as conferring a violence by assuming control over student and teacher subjectivities.

Introduction

Accountability is an important concept in the distribution and deployment of public resources, but questions exist over what kinds of accountability are appropriate and how evaluation of accountability should be conducted. Educational accountability of a technical kind is promoted globally in different ways to different extents through regimes of performativity, high-stakes testing and Datafication. Ranson argues that since the late 1970s in England, the education sector has been dominated by 'a regime of neo-liberal corporate accountability' (2003, p. 459). The aim, in the view of Stobart (2008), is to raise educational standards to meet the demands of the knowledge-based economy for enhanced human

---

This is an Open Access article distributed under the terms of the Creative Commons Attribution-NonCommercial-NoDerivatives License (http://creativecommons.org/licenses/by-nc-nd/4.0/), which permits non-commercial re-use, distribution, and reproduction in any medium, provided the original work is properly cited, and is not altered, transformed, or built upon in any way.

capital in an increasingly competitive international economic environment. Educational problems in England, such as declining standards, the attainment gap between advantaged and disadvantaged students and the nation's declining rank in international league tables, are signalled as resulting from poor levels of public education accountability (DfE, 2010a). Taking these discourses of policy problems/drivers at face value leads to the question of how to solve them. In other words, in an educational culture in which performance, expressed as measured productivity or output dominates as the key indicator of technical accountability, what policy levers and mechanisms exist by which the assumed policy problems may be resolved and educational performance thereby enhanced?

In the case of curriculum, policy levers summoned to solve educational accountability problems consist of the following: tightening curriculum control by means of a technical, 'one-size –fits all', standardized curriculum configuration (with prescribed outcomes), specification of curriculum knowledge, together with high-stakes standardized testing and statistical analysis and reporting. 'Datafication' (Lingard, 2011) or codification of assessment results in statistical form and allocation of borders assigning value to numerical scores serve as the means of evaluating whether or not the prescribed curriculum outcomes have been achieved, thereby signifying improved or declined student performance and hence configuring the basis of accountability judgements. The main argument of this paper is that the current dominance of technical accountability in curriculum is less than adequate because it overlooks educators' responsibility for ethical relations in responding to difference. Drawing on Levinasian thought, the paper explores teachers'/education stakeholders' experiences of curriculum in 'disadvantaged' English secondary schools in order to understand ethical relations arising when technical accountability dominates curriculum and assessment policy reform.

To contextualize the discussion, I begin by outlining three characteristics of the current technical accountability culture in education: performativity, high-stakes testing and datafication, before indicating the wealth of international critical policy research conducted in the field in the last 15 years. I turn next to explain the powerful influence of curriculum in constituting student (and teacher) subjectivities. Two conceptualizations of subjectivity that respond differently to warrants of technical accountability and ethical responsibility are examined in the paper's second part. In part 3, I present the methodology and analysis of data collected during an empirical enquiry into teachers/stakeholders' experiences of curriculum policy reform in English secondary schools. The fourth and concluding part of the paper returns the discussion to wider ethical implications of curriculum policy dominated by technical accountability.

Part 1: performativity, high-stakes testing and datafication

The rise of techniques and technology after World War 2, together with the flourishing of liberalism, with its economic focus and endorsement of the individual from the 1960s onwards, gave rise to a connection between technology and profit that marks the emergence of the concept of 'performative improvement' (Lyotard, 1984, p. 45). Performative improvement is achieved when technology follows the principle of minimization of input and maximization of output, in other words the 'best possible input-output equation' for optimal efficiency. Under the banner of efficiency, educational goals shift from universal narratives of truth, justice or beauty, to technical efficiency (ibid., p. 44). The objective is to optimize the education system's performance and therefore —it is presumed—under the operation of technical rationality, to maximize its accountability. Manifest in education systems via the drive to enhance productivity in order to meet the pragmatic needs of the economy by increasing the supply of functionally skilled workers, Ball describes performativity as:

> … a technology, a culture and a mode of regulation that employs judgements, comparisons and displays as a means of incentive, control, attrition and change—based on rewards and sanctions … The performances (of individual subjects or organisations) serve as measures of productivity or output, or displays of 'quality' or 'moments' of promotion or inspection. As such, they stand for, encapsulate or represent the worth, quality or value of an individual or an organisation within a field of judgement. (2003, p. 216)

Whilst the concept of performativity carries an aura of objectivity, certainty and transparency, its activities reduce complex social processes involved in the educational experience and the formation of subjectivities to codes, statistics and categories (Ball, 2003). Performativity provides a totalized audit mechanism within education systems by issuing examination scores, rankings, attainment indicators, levels of progress, assessment benchmarks and targets. An important procedure by which performativity is enacted is through the high-stakes testing of students, the primary aim of which is to raise standards of test and examination performance compared with national and other benchmarks and with other schools, through consistent, regular and frequent stock-taking (Barber, 2007). Comparison of students' examination scores forms a significant component of the performative education system, as individual students', school subjects', schools', Local Authorities' and nations' scores are ranked and borders are inserted between ranks to name and distinguish those individuals and institutions deemed to 'succeed' from those deemed to 'fail'. As part of the technical–rational accounting system, high-stakes testing is most efficiently managed using data.

Datafication forms a totalizing technical discourse governing the constitution, justification, implementation and evaluation of curriculum policy. Lingard (2011) explains how our complex post-Cold War world of 'ontological insecurity', formed through fundamentalist terrorism, neo-liberalism and new technologies, is seemingly rendered manageable via 'policy as numbers' techniques. These offer individuals, schools and nations what are assumed to be valid, reliable and therefore objective measures of accountability. Facilitated by technical advances in computing capacity and levels of analytical sophistication, datafication, on the one hand, allows people who want to be counted to be counted so that social inequalities can, seemingly, be identified and addressed through policy. On the other hand, datafication involves categorizing student and teacher subjectivities, in other words, codifying who and what people are (and even, what they will become), making them amenable to regulation and control, whilst at the same time hiding the technologies that conceptualize and constitute the data which, it is claimed, represent them (Rose, 1999). Datafication provides one form of educational accountability, but carries certain statistical requirements for codification and comparison, and, in turn, these require standardization of inputs, processes and outputs of the curriculum system. Examples include specified curriculum objectives and knowledge configuration, assessment criteria and benchmarks. Standardization facilitates codification for statistical representation and analysis, but can only be achieved by naming, defining and reducing meaning, in other words, 'fixing' meaning to fit system input, process and output requirements.

Educational accountability of the technical kind outlined above has been researched globally during the last 15 years, to form a rich collection of international critical policy scholarship. In the USA, researchers investigating the impact of 'test-based metrics' (Henig,

2013), mainly through theoretical (Au, 2008, 2011), metasynthesis (Au, 2007), national (Pedulla et al., 2003) or state-based enquiries, include Abrams (2004), Baker et al. (2010), Barrett (2009), Darling-Hammond (2010), Hursch (2013), Lipman (2013); and Perreault (2000). Examples of Australian contributions to the field range from global (Lingard, Martino, & Rezai-Rashti, 2013; Sellar and Lingard 2013) to national (Dulfer, Polesel, & Rice, 2012; Polesel, Rice, & Dulfer, 2014; Lingard, Sellar, & Savage, 2014; Lingard, 2011; Lingard & Sellar, 2013; Lingard, Creagh, & Vass, 2012) and state (Thompson, 2012) and finally school enquiries such as Comber (2012), Comber and Nixon (2009), Singh, Thomas, and Harris, (2013), Gerrard and Farrell (2013) and Keddie (2013). Recent English studies, such as Perryman (2006), Braun, Ball, Maguire, and Hoskins (2011), Ball, Maguire, Braun, and Hoskins (2011a, 2011b) and Maguire, Hoskins, Ball, and Braun (2011) focus on school policy enactment, with Ball (2003) and Leat, Livingston, and Priestley (2014) researching the national picture. Scholars who have ventured beyond structuralist and Foucauldian analytical perspectives, such as Sellar (2009, 2013) and Macedo (2013), consider the implications of technical accountability for social justice. But naming, defining (i.e. 'fixing') the words 'equality', 'equity', 'social justice' in school settings of complex, fluid human subjectivities runs up against issues of applying a totalizing economy on what are assumed to be calculable human subjects (Rose, 1999). By drawing on Levinasian ethics as a critical lens to interrogate student and teacher subjectivities under conditions of curriculum policy reform, this paper offers something innovative to the field of critical policy and curriculum studies.

The power of curriculum

The approach to standardization and associated tightening of control over curriculum practices through curriculum policy described above fits Lingard et al.'s (2013) proposal that increasingly, curriculum is understood by educational researchers 'as systemic policy ... implemented or enacted in schools and classrooms through pedagogy and framed by systemic evaluation, assessment and testing policies' (p. 549). Presupposing an interpretation of curriculum in a technical sense as specified knowledge content and objectives conveys an impression of objectivity and value-neutrality, whilst hiding curriculum's inevitable value-laden character. Likewise, in accordance with its Latin derivative 'currere' meaning 'a course to be run' (Cherryholmes, 2002, p. 116), curriculum establishes the seemingly unproblematic content and boundaries for what is included and excluded in the planned educational experience as well as expectations of future educational outcomes. Yet, enhancing the interpretation of curriculum above with Rizvi and Lingard's definition of policy as 'the authoritative allocation of values' (2010, p. 7) an alternative perspective arises. This alternative perspective recognizes curriculum policy as 'a cornerstone of educational governance' (Gerrard & Farrell, 2013, p. 4) because in addition to designating and legitimating official school knowledge, objectives, skills and assessment criteria, curriculum policy also influences pedagogical practices and relationships, the organization of school space and time (ibid.) and teacher and student meaning-making (Todd, 2001). As such, it forms a powerful totalizing mechanism over students' and teachers' experiences of education. Todd (2001) describes how curriculum is the 'raw material' of education and students may accept, reject or rewrite curriculum. In this sense, curriculum serves an important role in influencing student subjectivity. Education is one process by which the person becomes a subject or self. Curriculum, pedagogy and relationships constitute student subjectivity by influencing or shaping who and what students are and become. In the next part of the paper, I discuss two understandings of subjectivity and educational accountability/responsibility to inform the empirical enquiry to follow.

Part 2: two conceptualizations of subjectivity

Subjectivity and technical accountability

The modern Kantian conception of subjectivity and education is understood through the lens of humanism as the development of the rational, autonomous subject. The subject achieves autonomy, rationality and criticality through education (Biesta, 2010, p. 76), where the role of education is to release the learner from the binds of indoctrination and inculcation to bring out her/his potential as an autonomous subject with the free will to act rationally. The particular kind of human subject generated through this mode of thinking fits a humanist mould: 'the idea that it is possible to know and express the essence or nature of the human being, and also that it is possible to use this knowledge as the foundation for subsequent action' (Biesta, 2010, p. 78). Under Kantian humanism, being and becoming in the educational project is founded on a particular truth about what humans are and how they should act. The notion of humanness is specified in advance and education, under the spell of this specification becomes totalizing and reproductive. It governs educational discourses and blocks the emergence of alternative notions of being and becoming. Teaching is understood as sets of techniques or procedures used to deliver knowledge, values and reasoning skills into students' minds and souls to make autonomy possible (Biesta, 2010, p. 65) or, alternatively and according to the Socratic view of maieutics, teaching is about bringing the student into the world, as in the 'birth' of the knowledge and values that lie innate within the individual through the actions of the teacher-midwife (Strhan, 2012, p. 22).

Under the Enlightenment presumption that education guides the subject into an autonomous existence governed by reason lies the idea that the human subject, through education, becomes like me, another human subject. Thus, we are united in our humanness as members of the community of humans. Biesta explains one of the problems of this kind of thinking:

> … it posits a *norm* of humanness, a norm of what it means to be human, and in so doing excludes those who do not live up to or are unable to live up to this norm … this form of humanism … specifies a norm of what it means to be human *before* the actual manifestation of 'instances' of humanity. It specifies what the child, student or newcomer *must* become before giving them an opportunity to show who they are and what they will be. (Biesta, 2010, p. 79)

Difference is thereby suppressed and education adopts a reproductive role in normalizing what it means to be human.

An example of how the subject is inducted into the world of presence and sameness as an autonomous, rational individual is by means of the modern school curriculum. The standardized programme, or technical curriculum (Au, 2008, p. 505), consists of pre-defined objectives, prescribed knowledge configurations, such as core knowledge, competencies or concepts (Winter, 2011) and standardized assessment regimes. Such a curriculum centres round totalized discourses whereby knowledge becomes trapped or fixed in conceptual categories and language (Winter, 2009). These concepts can be, it is assumed, unproblematically defined and applied, outcomes of the educational endeavour judged and measured according to pre-specified criteria, leaving little space for alternative ways of thinking.

Curricula, under this approach, become controlling, driven by rationality and assumed clarity of meaning, rather than ethical (Eppert, 2008, p. 71). There is little scope within such curriculum discourses for questioning knowledge, concepts or the unstable meanings of words, in order to welcome the other. Prescription, standardization and assumed rigour preclude other ways of thinking, other ways of being. Conformity and calculability elide the singularity and uniqueness of the other (Todd, 2003a, p. 61).

Ball, Maguire, Braun, Perryman, and Hoskins (2012) describe regulatory regimes that are activated under the technical curriculum approach in the age of performativity as 'deliverology'. In the case of the English school system, the main focus of teaching, learning and relationships becomes the raising of predetermined standards as measured by the percentage of top examination grades. Key features of 'deliverology' include 'comprehensive' and 'accurate' assessment data on student achievement, target- and trajectory-setting, consistent, regular and frequent stock-taking and reporting and regular tracking of student progress (ibid., p. 514). Given the significance of raising standards of student achievement to the school's success and, in some cases, its survival, examination results become the main focus of attention for school staff. The language used to describe the emphasis on, even obsession with, grades by teachers in schools as 'bringing a lens to bear', 'a close-up view', 'bringing things into visibility' (ibid., p. 517) corresponds with the notion of the 'fix'. But this is not an innocent or neutral gaze, since the prime purpose of bringing everything into view is to know and categorize students according to the rules and mechanisms of the system. Policy naturalizes testing and reporting activities, valuing them as obvious and unquestionable and enlisting them in the service of achieving required ends, again, as dictated by the system. Echoing through the voices of teachers to be heard later in the paper, curriculum policy reform and its adjunct performativity produce new kinds of student and teacher subjectivities, relationships, new forms of human existence (Ball, 2003).

Subjectivity and ethical responsibility

Levinas's (1969) work challenges the modernist view of subjectivity and education, replacing it with a view of how humans become subjects through 'responsible subjectivity' arising from ethical human relationships. Arguing that ethics comes before everything—ethics is 'first philosophy' and 'a relation of responsibility to the other' (Strhan, 2012, p. 21) –the ethical relation to the other emerges from a pre-originary structure of being, beyond and before the invention of ontology. Levinasian ethics defies universalization and standardization because it is not bound by the kinds of totalizing discourses conferred by Enlightenment thinking, but goes beyond such philosophical programmes as 'an exterior relation to being, an otherwise than being' (Todd, 2003b, p. 2). Levinas wrote: '... pre-existing the plane of ontology is the ethical plane' (1969, p. 201). It is in the ethical relationship and through language that the subject comes into being. Subjectivity is constructed through the relation between the subject and the other. As a singular subject, I am summoned by a moral imperative presented by the other and I respond, taking responsibility for the other in such a way that is exterior or prior to any totalizing frameworks. Responsibility here is neither a rational relationship of exchange nor an understanding that the other should be brought into the totality of the same, that is, inducted into modernist frameworks of thought to make her like me, because this will deny her alterity, her difference. Instead, by listening to and being receptive to the otherness of the other, the other opens me by her demand to respond. I learn from and respond to her singularity, uniqueness and needs.

This way of thinking accepts that the subject has no pre-ordained nature or essence and that there exist no predetermined rules or frameworks (such as humanism) into which the subject should be inducted. Instead, understanding the distance, strangeness and separation between myself and the other and respecting the idea that selfhood comes from outside totalized philosophical programmes, from the exterior, 'brings me more than I contain' (Strhan, 2012, p. 23). The 'I' challenges the security and unity of the self as an interior being shaped by dominant discourses of domestication, destabilizing these structures and opening to an exteriority that has not been thought before. Levinas offers hope for a new and refreshed consideration of curriculum outside the boundaries of technical accountability. By challenging the assumed accurate and fixed meanings of words and numbers constituting discourses of performativity, high-stakes testing and datafication, by defying the constraining template of humanism, Levinas opens a space for thinking otherwise, unconstrained by externally prescribed specifications. His commitment to the ethical relation to the other drives our thinking beyond the dictates of the technical, beyond naming students using 'objective' criteria and reductive grades, ranking them in an hierarchy of 'success' and 'failure', fixing them to match some person's or group's ideas of what it means to be 'educated' and 'human', regardless of difference.

A change of tone of expression is required as I explain how the enquiry was conducted.

Part 3: the empirical enquiry

Methodology

The enquiry began as a meeting of geography and history teachers and education stake-holders to discuss responses to recent curriculum policy reforms. I invited colleagues to share views about General Certificate of Secondary Education (GCSE) attainment in local 'disadvantaged' secondary schools. I was interested to discover their perspectives on the current and future influence of recent policy reforms on GCSE geography and history examination performance. In England, student performance in GCSE examinations (usually taken by 16-year-olds) constitutes a significant indicator for accountability in national league tables. If less than 35% of pupils at the end of Key Stage 4 (KS4) achieve five or more GCSEs A*–C (or equivalents) including English and mathematics, then the school is considered to be 'under-performing' (DfE, 2010a).[1] Between 2012 and 2013, in one local authority in the north of England, although the percentage of top grades (>5 A*–C) rose in both low-and-high attaining non-selective state schools, the attainment gap between the two categories of schools remained at 25% over the same period. The meeting under discussion here was organized to plan, design and conduct collaborative research with practitioners and policy-makers, arising from issues identified and bearing potential for improving policy and practice. At the first meeting, five participants discussed the topic of 'GCSE attainment and education policy' in two groups (one group of three, the other of two; I joined the group of two), through 'inter-professional focussed conversations'.[2] The mix of professions in the groups ensured that practitioners and policy-makers talked directly with each other, making these groups different from individual interviews and focus groups with members with shared characteristics. I provided specific questions[3] in case the groups ran out of topics and the conversations were recorded. I later conducted face-to-face, semi-structured interviews with two Geography teachers who taught at the same 'disadvantaged' school as each other and had not participated in the first meeting. University ethical approval and participants' informed consent were obtained before any data collection began. Given the sensitivity of the topics under discussion, protection of participants' identities and institutions remains top priority.

Recordings were transcribed and a first-stage manual analysis took place using Braun & Clarke, 2006 approach, producing 28 initial codes which were collapsed into 15 themes. Following transcription of the individual interviews with two Geography teachers, second-stage analysis built on the first-stage codes and themes to produce 14 codes and three themes: performativity (7 codes), curriculum configuration (4) and academic culture (3). Reading and re-reading all the data revealed a recurring pattern of a normalization process of curriculum control through regulation and standardization. Closure, limits, rules, programmes, monitoring and surveillance technologies arose persistently in participants' accounts. Such systems of regulation and control illustrate the kind of totalizing discourses that Levinas calls us to overcome in order to open a space for thinking in which we retrieve our ethical responsibility to the other. During the second analysis stage, I followed Kierkegaarde's (1850, p. 357f) advice to 'go for a walk' in the data and the idea of the 'fix' emerged in the form of government intentions to 'mend' (repair, improve) the so-called unaccountable education system by 'dictating' (pinning down, defining, standardizing) certain ways of thinking, acting and being for students and teachers. In the final stage of analysis, I identified the concept of the 'fix' embedded within 14 (of the 15) themes and reorganized these in relation to three categories: curriculum, students and teachers. Member checks of transcript extracts to be included in this paper were carried out.

Although the number of participants was small, the meeting brought together colleagues with similar (they were all interested in the health of school geography and history), yet different (teachers and other stakeholders/policy-makers) professional interests in a relaxed and trusting atmosphere. I felt it important for teaching and non-teaching colleagues to listen to each others' perspectives (Coffield, 2012). The discussions were open and generative, providing an unexpected opportunity to gather data untethered from conventional semi-structured questions posed in individual or focus group interviews. Conversations were surprisingly frank and explanatory, as participants were compelled to explain their points to those of a different subject and professional stance. The meeting took place in a neutral space, away from participants' workplaces, and this, together with my expressed commitment to confidentiality seemed to dispel the perception of risk of accusations of disloyalty. Semi-structured individual teacher interviews took place later in the teachers' school. These were recorded, transcribed and analysed.

The analytical concept of the 'fix'

'Fix' is a slippery word. Every time I try to pin it down, it slides off in a different direction. I fix a light by replacing the bulb. I fix the dye of my jacket. The fixed price of an item in a shop means I cannot negotiate a discount. I fix my gaze on the bridge and then fix its location on the map. I sometimes get in a fix by failing to do something I promised to do. The British Prime Minister claimed that government policy would fix the country's education system (DfE, 2010a, Foreword), but I claim that government solutions are a stage-managed 'fix-up'.

The instability of word meanings illustrates how language defies accurate definition and totalization. I turn now to the interplay and non-presence of these meanings of the concept of 'the fix' which emerged from the analysis of the data. Data illustrate many ways in which curriculum policy operates as a driver of a technicalrational system of accountability through the imposition of frameworks of totalization. By compelling teachers and students to comply with its dictates, curriculum policy 'fixes' the knowledge configuration of the school curriculum, its structure and processes, at the same time as 'fixing' teachers and students as subjects.

Fixing curriculum, teachers and students

'Fixing' curriculum

Focus on specific subjects, core and content knowledge
Given the most important indicator of GCSE examination performance in English school league tables is the percentage of grades A*–C (including English and mathematics), these two subjects assume considerable significance in the high-stakes assessment regime. In attempts to increase students' grades, attention in participants' schools 'fixed' on the two specific curriculum subjects of literacy and numeracy, and, in the process, deflected from other subjects (Sahlberg, 2011, p. 100). For example, two primary teachers in one school were employed to withdraw students from the regular timetable to teach them literacy through phonics. Participants agreed that history and geography lost teaching time and status to literacy and numeracy, arguing that this had a detrimental effect because missed lessons meant declining performance in geography and history tests and students then decided not to study these subjects at GCSE. At the same time, a question is raised of the implications of basic technical skills in reading, writing and mathematics replacing an in-depth understanding of values and sensibilities of place, space and time conferred through geography and history.

The English Baccalaurate (E-Bac)[4] and core knowledge represent other 'fixes' on specific curriculum subjects. School E-Bac scores are published in examination league tables. At the time of its introduction, in order to qualify for an E-Bac, a student had to gain five or more top GCSE grades (A*–C) at in English language, mathematics, science, a foreign language and either history or geography. The E-Bac thus 'fixed' or privileged six traditional academic curriculum subjects and at the same time excluded more practical subjects such as art, design and technology, drama, food science, music, religious education and sports studies. The focus on a narrow range of academic subjects and knowledge 'missed the mark' in one participant's school:

> I fear it's a very one person or a small narrow group drive to make education fit their ideologies and their perception on what education should look like. For me it doesn't fit the skills base that's required out there ... the education system and the specifications that we're working towards ... seem to develop those that want a test in just academic ability, memory, just reading and writing. (Jo, teacher)

In 2010, the government announced that school curriculum knowledge was lacking in intellectual challenge, and it would introduce 'a tighter, more rigorous, model of the knowledge which every child should expect to master [*sic*] in core subjects at every key stage' (DfE, 2010a, para 11). 'Fixing' curriculum knowledge involves the identification and prescription of a bounded 'core' of disciplinary knowledge deemed to form the 'best' body of knowledge for the curriculum. It is defined and promoted as the knowledge that 'All children should acquire' (ibid., para 4.1) or ' ... be expected to master' [*sic*] (para 4.6); that all teachers should 'know how to convey effectively' (ibid., para 4.8) and against which students will be tested (para 4.2). This was experienced by teachers as an increase in the level of difficulty of the examination questions. Participants described this as 'a big shift in the culture of that GCSE'; 'more of an 'A' level slant to the ways the questions were worded'; 'they're drilling down in more narrow theoretical areas of Geography rather than the wider human-physical interactions' (Jo) and using 'more inference rather than explicit instruction you know, 'use a case study' would have been on a past paper, this one was 'here's the theory', but without telling the kids directly that they ought to apply the theory to the case study (Gordon, teacher). One participant remarked how the government had narrowed the curriculum to a core content:

> ... what's been happening is the notion of the core ... the way in which it's beginning to appear in Geography is that there's a notion of a body of content. For example at A-Level there's been fears going on for 20 years that it's possible to study an A-Level and veer away from the physical towards human and environmental geography. So, in order to address and correct that, what we're seeing is a core curriculum in effect or at least a core framework, saying there must be a balance of human and physical at GCSE and A-Level. (Graham, stakeholder)

Whilst the British government argues that a common core, disciplinary-based curriculum is socially just because it offers the same challenge to all, Yates (2009) suggests that an emphasis on 'the best that has been thought and said' (p. 22) fails to prepare students for a changing world and Zipin, Fataar, and Brennan (2015) argue that the rationale for disciplinary knowledge, by presenting the purpose of schooling to be cognition, thereby overlooks its ethical dimension.

Other 'fixes' were introduced via the raising of grade boundaries, replacement of modular with end-of-course examinations, the abolition of in-course resit examinations and of continuous assessment (Winter, 2014). This 'fixed' curriculum model was experienced first-hand by teacher participants in the subsequent examination period in a variety of practical ways: an increase in the number of examination questions without a proportionate increase in time available; in mathematics GCSE, a student had to achieve 12 more marks than the previous year to gain a grade C; vocational examinations which previously counted for 3–4 GCSE qualifications were redesigned to count for only one (Jo). Stakeholder David challenged the definition or fixing by examination boards of the correct historical knowledge for schools:

> In History we now have the chief examiner writing the textbook and all you need to know to pass the exam is in there. To me that runs absolutely counter to what History is about: discussion, disagreement, agreement, different sources and everything else. And so you might argue it's producing clarity but it's removing the professionalism of teachers. It's saying here are the answers, and there's no contesting these answers. In History the answers are never straightforward. And the chief examiner sets the paper, writes the book, does the CPD you know.

Reminiscent of Apple's idea of the teacher-proof 'curriculum on a cart', (Apple & Jungck, 2014, p. 136) such a programmatic engagement with knowledge arises through the assumed existence of right answers and the denial of complexity, multiple perspectives and other knowledge, even the unknowable. None the less, fixing school knowledge through examination specifications renders it more amenable to codification and commodification in the context of the need for efficiency and economy in the light of the privatization of examination boards.

'Levels of progress'

GCSE grades are of key significance in the English education system because they form the foundation for public performance tables. Students' target GCSE grades are calculated on the basis of 'levels of progress' (LPs) over the 5 years leading up to the GCSE examination. Primary school teachers assess their students in English, mathematics and science at age 11, just prior to moving to secondary school. These KS2 results are expressed as National Curriculum Attainment Levels (1–8 plus sub-levels A–C). DfE and Ofsted policy compel schools to aim to increase pupils' attainment by 3–4 levels between secondary school entrance at 11 and 16 years (GCSE, KS4). But GCSE grades are currently presented in the form of letter grades, so teachers use official 'transition matrices' to translate end of KS2 'levels' to GCSE target 'grades' (Ofsted/DfE, n.d.).

Problems arise with this system when primary school teachers focus on test preparation to maximize pupil performance for the published KS2 performance tables (Collins, Reiss, Stobart, & Collins, 2010). On entering secondary school, KS2 test scores form the basis for calculating target GCSE (KS4) grades, but as a result of teaching to the test, together with inadequacies in terms of validity of national testing (Stobart, 2008) in primary schools, pupils' target GCSE grades may be 'inflated' (Collins et al., 2010), and secondary school teachers face difficulties supporting pupils to meet target GCSE grades. This focus on levels of progress and GCSE grades illustrates a conundrum for teachers:

> I think the dilemma is now we have to show four levels of progress for our students to be classed as a 'Good School'. At the same time you've got that argument 'But we need to get the kids at five A*s to C'. So there are students who, on paper, will never get higher than an E or a D. Yet at the same time, as a department, you also need to try and get those Cs up. So even at four levels of progress it puts them at a D but as a department you still need them to get the A*s to C. (Frances, teacher)

One initiative recently introduced by both Ofsted and DfE (DfE, 2014) to monitor teachers regarding 'Progress Over Time' is for inspectors to examine students' books for evidence of progress through marking. Some schools interpret this policy as teachers marking every piece of work and one teacher identified marking workload as an issue:

> One of the things teachers are really struggling with at the moment is marking load. Because there is all this 'marking has to show impact'. So it's not that we've just marked your book, you have to see the impact for the kids. At the moment in a lot of schools everything has to be marked really in-depth. And you just can't do it. You just haven't got time. You can't spend five hours a night marking. (Claire, teacher)

Ball et al. (2011a, 2011b) acknowledge that teachers relate to and engage with policies in different ways in different contexts, yet, remarks above resonate with findings in their research schools, that teacher overload, time poverty and lack of autonomy are common occurrences.

Data management

The data management system in each school plays an important role in receiving, storing, analysing and delivering student data. At individual student level, in one participant's school, data are collected, stored, analysed and mined for reporting and intervention using the schools' management information system (SIMS). Data managers or teachers enter a host of data into the system, such as attendance, KS2 test levels, regular assessments, target GCSE grades, free school meals, behaviour, special educational needs, allergies, doctor's contact details and attitude to learning. In this school, data are then 'trawled', analysed and reported to parents three times per year for each year group except Yr 11 (the year in which students take their GCSE examination). Five 'trawls' take place for Yr 11 students. SIMS is not only used to predict and monitor academic progress, as a teacher participant explained:

> And then with this data, someone filters out all the people who've got a code, like code C for confidence and then they set up a nurture group where all the under-confident people can have some work on being confident. And all the ones whose attendance is poor, the attendance guys get to work on them. So you know, it's quite good at targeting support. (Gordon)

Hence, transparency is assured because students are 'known' through their metrics. A technical evidence base is important in order to demonstrate 'what works' and how to best achieve value and equity in schooling. Several problems arise with the assumption of transparency, however. First, the technical procedures involved in the metrics do not reveal or question the 'values internal to the logic of the testing regime' (Sellar, 2013, p. 6), nor the provenance of those values. Second, an assumption exists that human subjects can be comprehensively 'known' and domesticated into particular predetermined moulds through calculative processes. Third, such technical procedures have profound 'perverse effects' of promoting 'game-play' on the part of policy-makers in this high-risk endeavour (Lingard & Sellar, 2013) as well as misjudgement in assigning descriptors that form the basis of decision-making (Lingard et al., 2012).

At local and national levels, data comparison is a priority and schools in disadvantaged areas which recruit high levels of recently arrived migrant pupils seem to be 'punished' by the system relative to schools serving economically advantaged areas:

> Although it is rising, I think the current Year 11s[5], the average point score on entry [in this school-CW] is 24 point something and the average across the country is 27 point something. Those kids are likely to be less able to remember things. And yes, there are a lot of very intelligent students in this school, no doubt about it, some of the most able but there is a great proportion of lower ability and lower academically intelligent students that come in these doors. And what's my favourite figure this year? That Southview High had an intake in Year 7 of 89% Level 5s, so higher attainers, and we had an intake of 18.7% Level 5s. 10% of our whole school cohort are Roma and many of these arrived after the start of Year 9 straight from Slovakia and could not speak English and will not be able to attain perhaps even a G but will count towards the progress measures. So the school last summer achieved 54% A*- C, take 10% off that, 44% is what it would be if we were doing as well as we did last year. (Jo)

Teaching to the test

The curriculum, in the eyes of the participants, was not only narrowed by the importance conferred on literacy and numeracy, the E-Bac and core knowledge, but also as a result of the high-stakes testing regime driving students and teachers towards top GCSE grades. One teacher said: 'Because assessment drives the curriculum we're all teaching and people say 'don't teach towards the tests', but if you've got any sense you'll teach towards the tests because then your students will do better in the tests and they'll have better life chances. So it's the test that drives the curriculum' (Jo).

Research indicates a number of effects of high-stakes testing. For example, Polesel et al. (2014) cite: limitation on learning appropriate for the modern world (Au, 2008), promotion of shallow and superficial learning (Lobascher, 2011), 'cramming' for tests (Cunningham & Sanzo, 2002), shift to competitive and individualistic approaches (Reay & Wiliam, 1999), teachers operating as technicians (Hargreaves, 1994) and reduction in curriculum responsiveness to cultural difference (Klenowski, 2010, 2011). In the meeting, stakeholders focused on curbs to teacher creativity in content and pedagogy and student reactions. Frances remarked: 'the number of kids who say to me they really loved History at KS3, but 'if I'd have known it was going to be this at GCSE I wouldn't have done it'. Another teacher echoed this point with 'I think partly … lack of imagination … the kids are like: 'Miss, this is so boring'. Teachers regretted the decrease in their creativity, saying that lessons could be 'more organic and inquiry-based' and 'things that take that little bit more time perhaps are being done less and less' … 'because you're aware that you're being judged on data. So I think the key point is maybe the enriching side of things has taken a hit' (Gordon).

Participants described how pressure to support students to perform at a high level in GCSE necessitated the deployment of certain 'fixed' practices. David, stakeholder said: … the number of teachers I talk to who say the only way kids can do well at GCSE is to spend two or three years, every single lesson has to be one aspect of GCSE assessment. And it's death by exams. It's the tail wagging the dog' and a teacher spoke about stage-managed 'recipe-following' (Perryman, 2006, pp. 157, 158):

> Everything is very exam-driven. I think a lot is also driven by the inspection regime. Because if you're teaching a GCSE class and you don't model a GCSE answer and you don't talk about the difference between a C, a B, an A and an A* and you don't get them to do a self-assessment and peer assessment, you're given a poor lesson grade. (Claire)

The effect of the focus on examination targets and 'inspection-ready' lessons is to deflect teachers' attention and engagement from the wider goals and processes of education, as this teacher explains:

> But I think with the way you have to do things, you just don't think about the bigger picture do you? You can't think about what you've actually got because you've just got this end point that you're just drilling down to this end point of As to Cs, four LPs, you don't get time to have a look around and see what else you could do to get there. (Gordon)

'Fixing' teachers

One teacher responded to the question 'Is this data a good thing or … does it have a downside to it?' with the following:

> Well, as a subject leader it's a good thing. And I think as a classroom teacher it's a good thing. And as a parent it's a good thing. It's important to be able to measure progress that I want to know when I visit someone's class or someone visits my class: we want to know that there's an impact. It does have that perhaps unintended consequence of perhaps making the curriculum a little less creative and organic … because our eye is on the progress levels … because that's how teachers are being judged. (Gordon)

At the same time, he agreed with others in the group that teachers are in the firing line for blame if students' results do not meet predicted targets. Echoing Thompson and Cook (2014), participant teachers agreed that '… if your results are bad, you're made to feel like you're a bad person, never mind a bad teacher' (Claire). Such feelings arose amongst teachers in spite of recognition by senior staff of issues surrounding inappropriate designation of student targets, as discussed earlier:

> When you raise concerns about patterns raised in the data, off the record your line manager will often agree with you but when push comes to shove it's the way it is. You're made to feel that if you're disagreeing with the data it's because you've done something wrong, you've failed in

some way … rather than listening to your professional judgment of 'Well actually I don't know where that number's come from but that kid can't do it' and I think that's a real shame. (Claire)

She continued, remarking on the feelings of de-professionalization experienced under the recent policy reforms:

I do think that we're often not treated as professionals. A good example links back into the target-driven culture; there are kids whose targets are far too high … and even if that kid is trying, they're always highlighted red in our school. And every data collection that goes home, they're red, no matter what they do, they just can't reach that level.

Drawing attention to the ethical and political relations arising when parents receive regular reports from school of the failure of their child to 'make the grade', Claire describes her emotional responses to the persistent labelling of students in relation to a target:

I think that as a teacher, as a professional, the person who inputs that data should listen to me saying 'Look, that kid is not going to get that target; can you just bring it down? They are trying but just so that every single data collection that goes home, they're not coloured in red. It would just be a confidence boost for that child'. But they won't do it. And that upsets me because I'm not trying to do it to cop out, I'm not trying to do it so I don't have to work. But as a professional for me to be worried about that child, I think you should reduce their target, and it won't be done. And that I find insulting.

Claire was compelled to comply with policy against her professional and personal beliefs because these struck against what was perceived and prized as the needs of the learner and of the school. But since the official interpretation of learners' needs is caught up in the culture of technical accountability, teachers are complicit as government surveillance agents, 'deliverers' and reporters of curriculum policy, a role in which not only are their voices not heard, but their consciousness and consciences co-opted into a new agenda (Ball, 2003, p. 218).

'Fixing' students

Within the context of raising standards in disadvantaged schools, three issues relating to 'fixing' students arose. The first concerns how ways of thinking about students under a high-stakes assessment system adapt to fit the required discourse and output. A teacher remarked: '… I don't think you talk about students as students anymore, you talk about students as data'. Second, an 'economy of visibility' regarding student data profiles (Ball et al., 2012, p. 530) is evident in school policy, whatever emotional sensitivities it may confer:

For the kids with very high targets, there is a pressure to be continually achieving them and for the kids with very low targets, just how awful. Every GCSE class you walk into, you've got a sticker on the front of your book saying your target grade is G; what does that do for your self-confidence? (Claire)

The ethical implications of public humiliation through objectification, differentiation and labelling are overlooked in the drive to raise standards. Third, when asked whether he thought that students felt the pressure of targets and if so, what the effects might be, a teacher replied:

Sometimes you have to negotiate and you do get that look of resignation of children when you're just trying to squeeze that little bit more out of them, whether it's time or paragraphs. They've done a nice piece of work and you just say 'Do you know what your target is? It's a B; your four LPs is a B'. And they know what that means, so they know that we're under pressure to get that out of them. And yeah, it does maybe put a strain on the relationship every now and again. (Gordon)

Another form of 'fixing' students is evident in the ways the high-stakes system influences student access to specific subject choices (Hobbs, 2016). Given the pressure for schools to maximize their percentage of 5 or more A*–C grades, together with the introduction of a more intellectually challenging curriculum content and structure, a dilemma arises for teachers about which students they allow to study their subject at GCSE level. Teacher participants agreed that geography and history GCSE have come under tighter control as 'more academically-minded subjects', with 'large blocks of writing' that involve more 'independent thinking' than other subjects. As a result, they claimed that students with English as an additional language and the so-called 'lower ability' students were not keen or equipped to tackle the 'constant writing and research and being independent and asking the right questions and the higher order thinking that goes with it'. An important first issue arises that if levels of literacy and independent and academic thinking are considered to be student problems, then what responsibility rests with curriculum makers to construct, and with teachers to teach, a curriculum which is appropriate for students across a range of different characteristics. One stakeholder aptly remarked: 'If you've got nothing you want to read, why would you want to read? For a lot of children, you want something that they're interested in to read and write about' (David).

A second issue raised in the meeting limiting access to high-quality teaching in geography and history is how schools draw on non-specialist teachers at KS3 because the subject-qualified teachers are 'creamed off' to teach the high-stakes GCSE classes. Third, teachers recognized the dilemma presented in giving all students access to their subject:

> We had to look at the data of some of our students, so for example the ones that had taken History GCSE ... and there is a sheer panic in our History teacher's voice that she will not be able to get them the results that the school needs by the end of the two years. Should it stop a child doing it? Absolutely not. (Frances)

Under the performativity regime, however, the counter-argument from the schools' perspective was posed by a stakeholder:

> If you take the approach where everyone can have a go and it doesn't matter if you don't get a C, there are trade-offs in terms of, well, they could actually be doing another subject, where they could get a higher grade. (Jane)

The datafication of student identities makes students visible to others such that each is considered to be comprehensively known (albeit according to the predefined requirement of the system). Knowledge of students allows for their fine-grained differentiation, labelling and ranking around predetermined norms which are then used as a basis for distributing 'opportunity, dignity and esteem, both by attention to and neglect of the individual within systems of comparison, evaluation and documentation' (Ball et al., 2012, p. 530).

Conclusion

This paper investigates educators' experiences of curriculum policy reform in terms of its ethical relations under conditions of technical accountability. Participants draw attention to their everyday lived experiences whilst working under totalizing regimes that regulate their professional lives in ways that counteract their professional and ethical judgements, including practices involving the humiliation and coercion of students, teachers and parents. Levinas works beyond the constraints of the metaphysics of humanism, is concerned with the instability of language, totalizing discourses and ethical responsibility in relations of difference and thereby allows us to think outside a prescribed programme of technical accountability to see what or who is denied ethical relations when such a programme dominates the education system.

Some argue that education policies like the ones reported here are constructed by technocrats remote from the experiences of classrooms in disadvantaged schools (Coffield, 2012, p. 140) and unaware of the profound and reductive effects of analysing condensed student data to assess a limited range of skills across a student's school career (Polesel et al., 2014, p. 653). Nevertheless, policies heralding curriculum standardization, high-stakes testing and datafication conveniently deflect attention about and responsibility for educational accountability from government to teachers and thereby operate as what Lipman describes as 'coercive government' (2013, p. 558) at a time when disparagement of public services globally neatly propels the shift towards privatization. Lipman states: 'systems of accountability make education legible for the market and private appropriation, mark schools and school districts and pathological and in need of authoritarian governance, and justify minimalist schools in areas of urban disposability' (p. 558).

Complying with policy requirements also deflects attention from broader philosophical and ethical questions. The regulatory curriculum system locks students and teachers into a totalizing technical–rational framework in such an all-embracing way that spaces for considering, deliberating about and acting on ethical responsibilities for and to others are elided, screened away, hidden, denied. Conceptualizing education through pre-defined way of being, and understanding student and teacher subjectivities as available for moulding into prescribed forms seem not only illustrative of extreme hubris, but to confer violence on those compelled to engage as well as to close down a wide array of alternative ways of being. Although current dominant pre-defined curriculum standards and high-stakes assessment appear to offer rigorous educational accountability, a closer look finds practice lacking with regard to ethical responsibility. In other words, what the philosophical perspective and data in this paper illuminate is how the technical–rational discourse fails to address through its quest for pre-ordained order, the ethical importance of the singularity and uniqueness of the subject and of human relationality in education.

Education systems increasingly controlled and subject to surveillance through curriculum policy influence who teachers and students are and who they will become, in other words, their sense of self, their subjectivity. The dominant technical–rational curriculum system claims to be a comprehensive, high trust system for educational improvement. A closer look through the lens of a philosophical 'fix' reveals a deficit in ethical responsibility, brought about by the system's reliance on standardization, datafication and conformity around predetermined and externally imposed norms and neglecting alternative possibilities of being.

Notes

1. Also: below average % of pupils at the end of KS4 making expected progress in English (national median for 2010 = 72%); and below average % of pupils at the end of KS4 making expected progress in maths (national median for 2010 = 65%) (DfE, 2010b).
2. 'Inter-professional focussed conversations' form a development of Clough and Nutbrown's (2002, p. 84) 'focussed conversations' as the former were conducted in the study reported here with education stakeholders from different professional fields with interests in school geography and history curricula and assessment.

TEACHERS MATTER – BUT HOW?

3. (1) Is there a problem? (2) what are the problem/s? (3) what are the needs of students? (4) what are the needs of teachers? (5) what questions do we need to ask and answer?
4. The English Baccalaurate (E-Bac) is a performance indicator, i.e. a means of ranking schools in the GCSE examination league table.
5. Students aged 15–16 years.

Disclosure statement

No potential conflict of interest was reported by the author.

References

Apple, M. J., & Jungck, S. (2014). *Official knowledge: Democratic education in a conservative age* (3rd ed.). London: Routledge.

Abrams, L. M. (2004). *Teachers' views on high-stakes testing: Implications for the classroom.* Tempe, Arizona: Education Policy Research Unit College of Education Arizona State University EPSL-0401-104-EPRU.

Au, W. (2007). High-stakes testing and curricular control: A qualitative metasynthesis. *Educational Researcher, 36*, 258–267.

Au, W. (2008). Devising inequality: A Bernsteinian analysis of high-stakes testing and social reproduction in education. *British Journal of Sociology of Education, 29*, 639–651.

Au, W. (2011). Teaching under the new Taylorism: High-stakes testing and the standardization of the 21st century curriculum. *Journal of Curriculum Studies, 43*, 25–45.

Baker, E. L., Barton, P. E., Darling-Hammond, L., Haertel, E., Ladd, H. F., Linn, R. L., … Shepard, L. A. (2010). *Problems with the use of student test scores to evaluate teachers.* Unit Briefing Paper 278. Washington, DC: Policy Institute.

Ball, S. J. (2003). The teacher's soul and the terrors of performativity. *Journal of Education Policy, 18*, 215–228.

Ball, S. J., Maguire, M., Braun, A., & Hoskins, K. (2011a). Policy subjects and policy actors in schools: some necessary but insufficient analyses. *Discourse: Studies in the Cultural Politics of Education, 32*, 611–624.

Ball, S. J., Maguire, M., Braun, A., & Hoskins, K. (2011b). Policy actors: Doing policy work in schools. *Discourse: Studies in the Cultural Politics of Education, 32*, 625–639.

Ball, S. J., Maguire, M., Braun, A., Perryman, J., & Hoskins, K. (2012). Assessment technologies in schools: 'deliverology' and 'the play of dominations'. *Research Papers in Education, 27*, 513–533.

Barber, M. (2007). *Instruction to deliver: Tony Blair, the public services and the challenge of delivery.* London: Methuen.

Barrett, B. D. (2009). NCLB and the assault on teachers' professional practices and identities. *Teaching and Teacher Education, 25*, 1018–1025.

Biesta, G. J. J. (2010). *Good education in an age of measurement: Ethics, politics democracy.* London: Paradigm.

Braun, A., Ball, S. J., Maguire, M., & Hoskins, K. (2011). Taking context seriously: Towards explaining policy enactments in the secondary school. *Discourse: Studies in the Cultural Politics of Education, 32*, 585–596.

Braun, V., & Clarke, V. (2006). Using thematic analysis in psychology. *Qualitative Research in Psychology, 3*, 77–101.

TEACHERS MATTER – BUT HOW?

Cherryholmes, C. H. (2002). Curriculum ghosts and visions: and what to do? In W. E. Doll & N. Gough (Eds.), *Curriculum visions* (pp. 116–129). Oxford: Peter Lang.

Clough, P., & Nutbrown, C. (2002). *A student's guide to methodology*. London: Sage.

Coffield, F. (2012). Why the Mc Kinsey reports will not improve school systems. *Educational Researcher, 36*, 258–267.

Collins, S., Reiss, M., & Stobart, G. (2010). What happens when high-stakes testing stops? Teachers' perceptions of the impact of compulsory national testing in science of 11-year-olds in England and its abolition in Wales. *Assessment in Education: Principles, Policy and Practice, 17*, 273–286. 10.1080/0969594X.2010.496205

Comber, B. (2012). Mandated literacy assessment and the reorganisation of teachers' work: Federal policy, local effects. *Critical Studies in Education, 53*, 119–136.

Comber, B., & Nixon, H. (2009). Teachers' work and pedagogy in an era of accountability. *Discourse: Studies in the Cultural Politics of Education, 30*, 333–345.

Cunningham, W., & Sanzo, T. (2002). Is high-stakes testing harming lower socio-economic schools? *National Association of Secondary School Principals (NASSP) Bulletin, 86*, 62–75.

Darling-Hammond, L. (2010). *The flat world and education: How America's commitment to equity will determine our future*. New York, NY: Columbia University: Teachers' College Press.

DfE. (2010a). *The importance of teaching: The schools white paper*. Cm 7980. London: Her Majesty's Stationery Office.

DfE. (2010b). School performance tables 2010 Expected levels of secondary school performance. Retrieved May 8, 2016, from http://www.education.gov.uk/schools/performance/archive/schools_10/s2.shtml#expectedlevels

DfE. (2014). *Key stage 2 – Key stage 4 progress measures*. file:///C:/Users/Chris/Downloads/Guide_to_KS2-KS4_progress_measures_2014[1]%20(1).pdf.Retrieved January14, 2016, from http://www.education.gov.uk/schools/performance/archive/schools_10/s11.shtml

Dulfer, N., Polesel, J., & Rice, S. (2012). *The experience of education: The impacts of high-stakes testing on school students and their families: An educator's perspective*. Sydney: Whitlam Institute University of Western Sydney.

Eppert, C. (2008). Emmanuel Levinas, literary engagement and literature education. In D. Egea-Khuehne (Ed.), *Levinas and education* (pp. 67–84). London: Routledge.

Gerrard, J., & Farrell, L. (2013). 'Peopling' curriculum policy production: researching educational governance through institutional ethnography and Bourdieuian field analysis. *Journal of Education Policy, 28*(1), 1–20.

Hargreaves, A. (1994). *Changing teachers changing times: Teachers' work and culture in the post-modern age*. London: Cassell.

Henig, J. R. (2013). Foreword. In D. Anagnostopoulos, S. A. Rutledge, & R. Jacobsen (Eds.), *The Infrastructure of accountability: Data use and the transformation of American Education*. Cambridge, MA: Harvard Education Press. vii–xiii.

Hobbs, K. (2016). *The constitution and implementation of the English Baccalaureate: Implications for educational equality* (Unpublished EdD thesis). Sheffield: University of Sheffield School of Education.

Hursh, D. (2013). Raising the stakes: High-stakes testing and the attack on public education in New York. *Journal of Education Policy, 28*, 574–588.

Keddie, A. (2013). Thriving amid the performative demands of the contemporary audit culture: A matter of school context. *Journal of Education Policy, 28*, 750–766.

Kierkegaarde, S. (1850). *Letter*. 263. p. 357f. April, 1850 to Emile Boesen. Retrieved from http://sorenkierkegaard.org/kierkegaard-letters-documents.html

Klenowski, V. (2010, November 10–15). Are Australian assessment reforms fit for the purpose: Lessons from home and abroad. *Queensland Union of Teachers Professional Magazine*, 10–15.

Klenowski, V. (2011). Assessment for Learning in the accountability era: Queensland Australia. *Studies in Educational Evaluation, 37*, 78–83.

Leat, D., Livingston, K., & Priestley, M. (2014, October). *Curriculum deregulation in England and Scotland: Different directions of travel?* Conference presentation 'Do Teachers Matter; but how?' Linnaeus University, Vaxjo, Sweden.

Levinas, E. (1969). *Totality and infinity: An essay on exteriority*. (A. Lingis, Trans.). Pittsburgh, PA: Duquesne.

Lingard, B. (2011). Policy as numbers: Ac/counting for educational research. *The Australian Educational Researcher, 38*, 355–382.

Lingard, B., Creagh, S., & Vass, G. (2012). Education policy as numbers: Data categories and two Australian cases of misrecognition. *Journal of Education Policy, 27*, 315–333.

Lingard, B., Martino, W., & Rezai-Rashti, G. (2013). Testing regimes, accountabilities and education policy: Commensurate global and national developments. *Journal of Education Policy, 28*, 539–556.

Lingard, B., & Sellar, S. (2013). 'Catalyst data': Perverse systemic effects of audit and accountability in Australian schooling. *Journal of Education Policy, 28*, 634–656.

Lingard, B., Sellar, S., & Savage, G. C. (2014). Re-articulating social justice as equity in schooling policy: The effects of testing and data infrastructures. *British Journal of Sociology of Education, 35*, 710–730.

Lipman, P. (2013). Economic crisis, accountability, and the state's coercive assault on public education in the USA. *Journal of Education Policy, 28*, 557–573.

Lobascher, S. (2011). What are the potential impacts of high-stakes testing on literacy education in Australia? *Australian Journal of Language and Literacy, 34*, 9–19.

Lyotard, J.-L. (1984). *The postmodern condition: A report on knowledge*. (G. Bennington and B. Massumi, Trans.). Manchester, NH: Manchester University Press.

Macedo, E. (2013). Equity and difference in centralized policy. *Journal of Curriculum Studies, 45*, 28–38.

Maguire, M., Hoskins, K., Ball, S. J., & Braun, A. (2011). Policy discourses in school texts. *Discourse: Studies in the Cultural Politics of Education, 32*, 597–609.

Ofsted/DfE. (n.d.). *Transition matrices* (RAISEonline). Retrieved January 14, 2016, from https://www.raiseonline.org/documentlibrary/ViewDocumentLibrary.aspx

Pedulla, J. L., Abrams, L. M., Madaus, G. F., Russell, M. K., Ramos, M. A., & Miao, J. (2003). *Perceived effects of state-mandated testing programs on teaching and learning: Findings from a national survey of teachers*. National Board on Educational Testing and Public Policy. Boston, MA: Lynch School of Education, Boston College.

Perreault, G. (2000). The classroom impact of high-stress testing. *Education, 120*, 705–710.

Perryman, J. (2006). Panoptic performativity and school inspection regimes: Disciplinary mechanisms and life under special measures. *Journal of Education Policy, 21*, 147–161.

Polesel, J., Rice, S., & Dulfer, N. (2014). The impact of high-stakes testing on curriculum and pedagogy: A teacher perspective from Australia. *Journal of Education Policy, 29*, 640–657.

Ranson, S. (2003). Public accountability in the age of neo-liberal governance. *Journal of Education Policy, 18*, 459–480.

Reay, D., & Wiliam, D. (1999). 'I'll be a nothing': Structure, agency and the construction of identity through assessment. *British Educational Research Journal, 25*, 343–354.

Rizvi, F. & Lingard, B. (2010). *Globalizing education policy*. London: Routledge.

Rose, N. (1999). *Powers of freedom*. Cambridge: Cambridge University Press.

Sahlberg, P. (2011). *Finnish lessons: What can the world learn from educational change in Finland?*. New York, NY: Teachers' College Press.

Sellar, S. (2009). The responsible uncertainty of pedagogy. *Discourse: Studies in the Cultural Politics of Education, 30*, 347–360.

Sellar, S. (2013). Transparency and opacity: Levinasian reflections on accountability in Australian schooling. *Educational Philosophy and Theory, 47*, 118–132.

Sellar, S., & Lingard, B. (2013). The OECD and global governance in education. *Journal of Education Policy, 28*, 710–725.

Singh, P., Thomas, S., & Harris, J. (2013). Recontextualising policy discourses: A Bernsteinian perspective on policy interpretation, translation, enactment. *Journal of Education Policy, 28*, 465–480.

Stobart, G. (2008). *Testing times: The uses and abuses of assessment*. London: Routledge.

Strhan, A. (2012). *Levinas, subjectivity, education: Towards an ethics of radical responsibility*. Oxford: Wiley-Blackwell.

Thompson, G. (2012). *Effects of NAPLAN. Executive summary*. Murdoch, Perth: Murdoch University.

Thompson, G., & Cook, I. (2014). Education policy-making and time. *Journal of Education Policy, 29*, 700–715.

Todd, S. (2001). Bringing more than I contain': Ethics, curriculum and the pedagogical demand for altered egos. *Journal of Curriculum Studies, 33*, 431–450.

Todd, S. (2003a). *Learning from the other: Levinas, psychoanalysis and ethical possibilities in education*. New York: University of New York Press.

Todd, S. (2003b). Introduction: Levinas and education: The question of implication. *Studies in Philosophy and Education, 22*, 1–4.

Winter, C. (2009). Places, spaces, holes for knowing and writing the earth: The Geography curriculum and Derrida's *Khora. Ethics and Education, 4*, 337–354.

Winter, C. (2011). Curriculum knowledge and justice: Content, competency and concept. *Curriculum Journal, 22*, 337–364.

Winter, C. (2014). Curriculum knowledge, justice, relations: The Schools' White Paper (2010) in England. *Journal of Philosophy of Education, 48*, 276–292.

Yates, L. (2009). From curriculum to pedagogy and back again: Knowledge, the person and the changing world. *Pedagogy, Culture and Society, 17*, 17–28.

Zipin, L., Fataar, A., & Brennan, M. (2015). Can social realism do social justice? Debating the warrants for curriculum knowledge Selection. *Education as Change, 19*, 9–36.

Accountability and control in American schools*

Richard M. Ingersoll and Gregory J. Collins

ABSTRACT

One of the most controversial and significant of contemporary education reforms has been the teacher accountability movement. From this perspective, low-quality teachers and teaching are a major factor behind inadequate school performance, and a lack of accountability and control in schools is a major factor behind the problem of low-quality teachers and teaching. In turn, to advocates of this reform movement, the solution is to centralize control of schools and hold teachers more accountable. Utilizing a sociology of organizations, occupations and work perspective, the objective of this article was to offer a critique of the teacher accountability perspective and movement. This article draws from, and summarizes, the results of a series of empirical research projects on the levels, distribution and effects of accountability and control in American schools. The argument of the article is that the teacher accountability perspective overlooks some of the most important sources and forms of organizational accountability and control that exist in schools and overlooks the ways schools themselves, and in particular the ways they are managed and organized, contribute to the teacher quality problem. As a result, teacher accountability reforms often do not succeed and can have a negative impact on teacher quality and school performance.

Few educational issues have received more attention in recent times than the problem of ensuring that elementary and secondary classrooms are staffed with quality teachers. This concern is unsurprising—elementary and secondary schooling is mandatory in most nations and it is into the care of teachers that children are legally placed for a significant portion of their lives. The quality of teachers and teaching is undoubtedly among the most important factors shaping the learning and growth of students. Moreover, typically the largest single component of the cost of education is teacher compensation. Across nations, a seemingly endless stream of commissions and national reports has targeted improving teacher quality as one of the central challenges facing schools. In the USA, critics have blamed the perfor-mance of teachers for myriad social ills: the erosion of American economic competitiveness, the decline in student academic achievement, teenage pregnancy, juvenile delinquency, a decline in morals, gender and racial stereotyping and discrimination, and on and on (for

---

*An earlier version of this paper was presented at *Teachers Matter—But How?* an International Research Conference held at Linnaeus University, Vaxjo, Sweden, October, 2014. This manuscript is submitted as part of a special issue, entitled 'Teachers Matter'.

examples or reviews, see, Bennett, 1993; Goldstein, 2015; Levin, 1998; Moulthrop, Calegari, & Eggers, 2005; Sadker & Sadker, 1994; Santoro, 2011; Thomas & Wingert, 2010; Urban League, 1999). As a result, in recent decades, a host of initiatives seeking to upgrade teacher quality has been pushed by reformers across the USA and other nations.

Although ensuring that classrooms are all staffed with quality teachers is a perennially important issue in schools, in our view, it is also among the least understood. This misunderstanding centres on the reasons behind the purportedly low quality of teachers and teaching in schools, and it has undermined the success of reform efforts. Behind the criticism and reforms are a variety of differing perspectives as to the sources of the problems plaguing the teaching occupation.

In the USA, one of the most popular perspectives relates to the accountability and control of teachers in schools. Schools, this view claims, are marked by low standards, poor management and little effort to ensure adequate supervision, especially in regard to their primary activity—the work of teachers with students. Given the nature of teachers' work, such concern is understandable. Not only do schools instruct students in reading, writing and arithmetic, but they are also a major mechanism for the socialization of children, a process captured in the concept of social capital (Coleman, 1987; Grant, 1988). The task of deciding which behaviour and values are proper and best for the young is not trivial, neutral or value-free. Hence, it is no surprise that those who do this work—teachers—and how they go about it, are matters of intense concern. Indeed, underlying the accountability perspective is the understandable assumption that education is too important to be left, solely, up to educators. From the teacher accountability perspective, the assumption is that teachers are often not held accountable and simply do what they want behind the closed classroom doors. The predictable result, this view holds, is low-quality performance on the part of teachers and students (e.g. Elmore, 2000; Finn, Kanstoroom, & Petrilli, 1999; Thomas & Wingert, 2010).

For those who subscribe to this teacher accountability perspective, the obvious route to improvement is to further centralize control of schools and to hold teachers more accountable; in short, to 'tighten the ship.' Proponents of this perspective advocate mechanisms of enhanced organizational control, such as teacher examinations, standardized curricula and especially the implementation of explicit performance standards, coupled with more rigorous teacher evaluation.

A prominent focus of the teacher accountability perspective and reform movement in the USA is to change the traditional ways that teachers have been evaluated, and rewarded, in regard to employment decisions about teacher hiring, lay-offs, promotions and salary (e.g. National Council on Teacher Quality, 2010; New Teacher Project, 2010). The traditional public school approach in the USA bases these decisions primarily on measures of teachers' qualifications, including years of experience, degrees completed and types of licensure. Many accountability proponents deny the existence of a strong link between these traditional measures of qualifications and the actual performance of teachers, in turn, pushing to replace the former with new approaches that better capture teacher quality. A variety of methods have been developed and implemented, such as the controversial 'value-added' model, which attempts to assess teachers by measuring gains in their students' test scores (Hershberg, 2005).

The theory of action behind teacher accountability-based reforms posits a series of sequential steps: establishing performance standards for teachers, utilizing assessments,

TEACHERS MATTER – BUT HOW?

Step 1		Step 2		Steps 3 & 4	Step 5
Set Teacher Performance Standards	→	Assess Teacher Performance on Standards	→	Pass Assessments – Rewards Fail Assessments – Sanctions →	Improve Teacher Performance

Figure 1. The theory of educational accountability.

often students' standardized test scores, to gauge student and teacher performance in regard to the standards, and instituting incentives and sanctions to induce teacher improvement (see Figure 1). Many of these mechanisms have become widely used in the USA since the advent of the federal No Child Left Behind Act in 2002. Often underlying this theory of action is what might be called a 'teacher-deficit' assumption. In this assumption, the primary source of low-quality teaching in schools lies in various deficits in teachers themselves—their ability, commitment or effort. The best way to fix schools, it is then argued, is to fix these deficits in individual teachers through increased regulations, incentives and sanctions.

A lack of accountability and control is, of course, not the only explanation given for the problem of low-quality teachers and teaching. But it is a prominent view in the USA and across many nations and has had an increasing impact on reform and policy.

Objectives

The teacher accountability perspective and its reforms have been the subject of a growing body of criticism—from a variety of perspectives, and focused on a variety of aspects of the theory underlying accountability, the reforms it has spawned and the outcomes it has engendered. In this article, we add another critique of this teacher accountability perspective, utilizing an unusual theoretical perspective—one drawn from the sociology of organizations, occupations and work. Our operating premise is that fully understanding issues of teacher quality requires examining the character of the teaching occupation, and the character of the organizations in which teachers work. Unlike the teacher-deficit viewpoint, this perspective seeks to illuminate the ways the organizational conditions of schools, and the conditions of the teaching occupation, contribute to the problem of teaching quality.

In particular, we focus on the distribution, mechanisms and effects of control and power in schools. Our argument is that the teacher accountability perspective overlooks some of the most important sources and forms of organizational accountability and control that already exist in schools and, as a result, overlooks the ways school management and organization contribute to the teacher quality problem. In plain terms, our argument is that poorly-run schools can make otherwise excellent teachers not so excellent.

Our view is that proponents of the teacher accountability perspective identify important issues and problems. Accountability in schools is reasonable and necessary, and the public has a right and, indeed, an obligation to be concerned with the performance of teachers. There is no question that some teachers are poorly performing and inadequate for the job, in one way or another. Our argument, however, is that the teacher accountability perspective involves a flawed diagnosis of the source of teacher quality problems and hence offers inadequate prescriptions to fix such problems. As a result of a partial, one-sided explanation of the source of teacher quality problems, we argue, teacher accountability reforms often do not work and can even make things worse.

This article does not report in detail on a single empirical study of accountability and control in schools. Rather, it bolsters our above argument by synthesizing the results of a series of research projects we have undertaken over the past two decades on the levels, distribution and effects of accountability and control in American schools (Ingersoll, 2003, 2004, 2012; Ingersoll & Merrill, 2011; Ingersoll, Merrill, & May, in press). Throughout this article, we update our earlier findings with the most recent data available. We focus on schools in the USA, but our view is that this is but one case in a growing international trend.

Our objective is to address three sets of questions:

(1)   *Who controls teachers work?*

How does the distribution of control in the USA educational system compare to that in other nations? Are schools highly centralized organizations, or are they more participatory and decentralized workplaces? Do teachers have influence equivalent to that of traditional professionals, or more like that of lower-level employees?

(2)   *What is the balance between teachers' responsibilities and teachers' control?*

What is the role of teachers in schools, especially in regard to the degree of responsibility and accountability required of them, and the degree of control and power delegated to them?

(3)   *What difference does teacher control make?*

What difference does the amount of centralization or decentralization in schools make for how well schools function? What effect does the amount of teacher influence and control have on life inside schools?

In the next section, we briefly describe the data and concepts we have utilized in our research projects. Then, we interpret our results to answer the three research questions. We close by discussing the implications of our data for the accountability perspective and suggest an alternative approach to school organization that attempts to balance the needs for both organizational accountability and employee autonomy and control.

Data and concepts

In this article, we rely on analyses of a wide array of data, both qualitative and quantitative. The primary data for these studies were from the nationally representative Schools and Staffing Survey (SASS), along with its supplement, the Teacher Follow-up Survey (TFS). SASS/ TFS is the largest and most comprehensive data source available on elementary and sec-ondary school teachers in the USA. The National Center for Educational Statistics (NCES), along with the US Census Bureau, periodically collect the SASS data from a random sample of schools stratified by state, public/private sector and school level (National Center for Education Statistics, 2011–2013). Each SASS cycle includes questionnaires for a random sample of teachers in each school and for school-level and district-level administrators. In addition, after 12 months, the same schools are again contacted, and all those in the original teacher sample who had left their teaching jobs are given a second questionnaire to obtain information on their departures. This latter group, along with a representative sample of those who stayed in their teaching jobs, comprise the TFS. To date, seven SASS/TFS cycles have been conducted between 1987 and 2013 (for more information on SASS, see Goldring, Gray, & Bitterman, 2013; for more information on TFS, see Graham, Parmer, Chambers, Tourkin, & Lyter, 2011).

Another source of data for our research was the Organisation for Economic Co-operation and Development (OECD). OECD is a leading international research and development organization and one of the best sources of international data on education. A series of studies of school control and governance has been conducted by the OECD—beginning in 1990–1991 with The International Survey of the Locus of Decision-Making in Educational Systems, and since 2000, as part of the Programme for International Student Assessment (PISA). The objective of these surveys has been to ascertain the extent of centralization of the elementary/secondary educational systems in different nations. These surveys focused several key decisions, concerned with both educational and administrative activities, that could conceivably be made at a school or school board level. They then determined whether these decisions were indeed made at a local level or at higher levels of governance.[1] For instance, the PISA 2012 survey asked school administrators to report whether the teachers, the school principal, the school's governing board, regional/state education authorities or the national/federal education authority had substantial responsibility for 12 key tasks, such as determining school budgets, establishing curriculum and teacher hiring (OECD, 2013). We also present OECD comparative data on teacher salaries drawn from the Indicators of Education Systems (INES) project (OECD, 2014).

In the debate over accountability and control, confusion arises because different analysts use different definitions for the same phenomena or use similar definitions for different phenomena. Hence, it is necessary to clarify our usage of key concepts and terms. The hierarchical distribution of power lies at the crux of the above-discussed larger debates concerning school accountability and is the focus of this article. Among researchers and commentators, power and related concepts—control, autonomy, influence—have been defined in a variety of ways. Drawing from an organizational sociology perspective, power as we define it here is synonymous with control; it is a relationship wherein an individual or group influences or controls particular issues or decisions.[2]

In this article, we will examine several levels of decision-making and look at the control over teachers' work held at these different levels. But the primary focus is the control held by teachers themselves over the terms and content of their work, both individually and collectively, both school-wide and within classrooms, and for both academic and non-academic issues. In this article, school centralization or decentralization refer to the relative levels of power and influence of two groups—teachers and administrators—*within* schools. Hence, when we refer to a decentralized school, we mean one in which there is a great deal of teacher control—where teachers hold a lot of control over their work relative to school administrators. A centralized school, on the other hand, is one in which there is a great deal of organizational control—where school and district administrators hold a lot of control over teachers' work relative to teachers themselves.

Results

Who controls teachers' work?

In contrast with most European nations, public schooling in the USA originally began on a highly democratized, localized basis. The resulting legacy is a current system of some 13,500 individual public school districts, governed by local school boards of citizens, each with legal responsibility for the administration and operation of publicly - funded, universal, mandatory elementary and secondary schooling (Tyack, 1974). Local school districts in the USA are clearly no longer the autonomous bodies they once were. Over the past half century, myriad other organizational actors have increasingly exerted, or sought to influence, control of schooling, including state governments, external pressure groups, the judicial system and the federal government (Kirst, 1984). Beginning in 2002, there was an unprecedented expansion of the federal role in education through the No Child Left Behind Act. Nevertheless, comparative data from the above-described OECD surveys indicate that, despite these changes, schooling in the USA still remains a far more nonfederal and local affair than in most other countries.

The OECD data show that, since the early 1990s, numerous nations have decentralized their educational decision-making from federal to local levels. In contrast, for the USA, the data show a growth of control exercised at the federal level and especially the state level. Despite this, the USA still has an unusually small proportion of important educational decisions made at the federal level, and an unusually large proportion made at the school or local school board levels. As illustrated in Figure 2, of the decisions included in the 2012 survey, in the USA, only 2% were made at the federal level, while 70% were made at the local level or below. These data do not mean schools are entirely autonomous, as rarely does the school have sole authority for decisions. However, at a systemic level, the international data do indicate that control of schooling in the USA remains relatively decentralized.

When we focus on the distribution of power within schools themselves, a different picture emerges. While the education system in the USA is relatively decentralized, schools themselves are not. As shown in Figure 2, US teachers are less likely to have influence over key decisions, relative to teachers in many other nations, and relative to their schools' principals. In other words, the OECD data show that while many key decisions in the USA are made locally, these are controlled far more often by school administrators than by teachers.

The degree of power and control practitioners hold over decisions in their workplaces is one of the most important criteria sociologists of organizations, occupations and work have used to distinguish the degree of professionalization in a particular line of work (e.g. Freidson, 1986; Hodson & Sullivan, 1995). Professionalized employees usually have control and autonomy approaching that of senior management when it comes to organizational decisions surrounding their work. University professors, for example, often have equal or greater control than that of university administrators over the content of their teaching and research, over the hiring of new colleagues, over the evaluation and promotion of members through peer review, and, hence, over the ongoing content and character of their profession. Members of lower-status occupations usually have less say over their work.

This portrait from the OECD data of a high degree of centralization within schools across the USA is further supported by our analyses of the SASS data. Our research has documented that in comparison with traditional professions, and relative to school administrators, teachers on average have only limited power and control over key decisions concerning the

TEACHERS MATTER – BUT HOW?

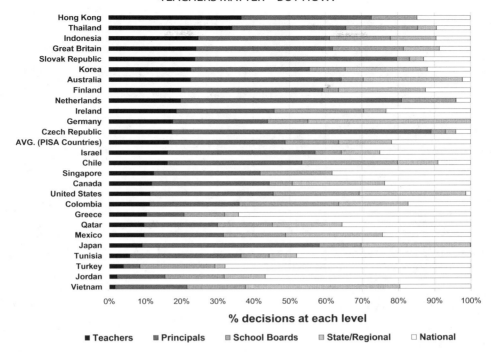

Figure 2. International differences in the control of schools: percentage of key decisions made at different levels of educational systems, 2012. Data source: OECD (2013). *Programme for International Student Assessment (PISA)*.

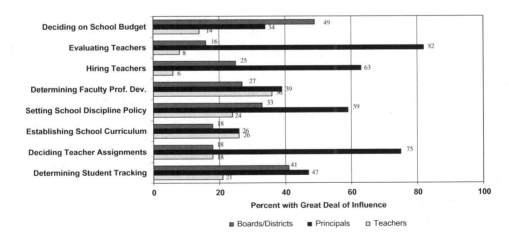

Figure 3. The relative influence of school boards, principals and teachers, over key school decisions, 1990–1994. Source: Ingersoll (2003).

day-to-day management of their work and their workplaces (Ingersoll, 2003). This is illustrated in Figures 3 and 4, which present US national data for two points in time (the early 1990s and 2011–2012) of the relative influence of teachers and administrators (note: the earlier SASS surveys included items on the influence of school boards and districts; in 2011–2012, such data were not collected). As Figures 3 and 4 illustrate, at the top of the hierarchy

TEACHERS MATTER – BUT HOW?

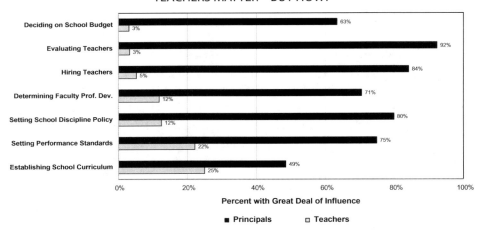

Figure 4. The relative influence of principals and teachers over key school decisions, 2011–2012. Data Source: 2011–2012 Schools and Staffing Survey.

within schools, for most of the school decisions examined, lie principals. At the bottom of the hierarchy, for most of the decisions, lie teachers.[3,4]

A key example of the imbalance of control between teachers and administrators is the area of teacher hiring and evaluation. The hiring and evaluation of colleagues is an area for which professionals traditionally have a great deal of control. University professors, for example, typically have equal or more influence, relative to university administrators, over hiring and promotion decisions.[5] This does not hold for elementary and secondary school teachers in the USA.

Moreover, as illustrated in Figure 3, principals also have the prerogative to decide teachers' course assignments, directing the subjects, courses and grade levels they will teach. This issue lies at the heart of the professional status of any occupational group. It is a crucial issue for teachers because it reveals the extent to which teachers lack control over the content of their jobs and also because of its implications for their degree of expertise. Our research has documented that out-of-field teaching—teachers assigned to teach subjects which do not match their fields of preparation—is widespread in the USA (Ingersoll, 1999, 2004). This misassignment, which may be responsible for some of the negative perceptions of teacher quality, lies largely out of teacher control.

Also striking are administrator/teacher differences in control over decisions regarding school curricula. This is another issue for which professors typically have equal or more influence, relative to college and university administrators. The data show that most teachers have limited control over the school's instructional programme. As illustrated in both Figures 3 and 4, only about a quarter of school faculties exert a great deal of actual influence over decisions concerning establishing the overall school curriculum.

A similar account holds for teachers' influence over important decisions regarding the clients they serve—students. In the case of determining the school's discipline policy, a crucial part of student socialization, far fewer teachers than principals reported having substantial control. Likewise, as shown in Figure 3, teachers often had little say over what kind of student ability grouping the school has and which students are placed into which tracks or ability levels. Our fieldwork (Ingersoll, 2003) further revealed that teachers typically had little say over decisions surrounding whether to promote particular students or require them to repeat a grade. Likewise, teachers had little influence over the assignment of students to their courses. In addition, rarely did teachers have the power to remove disruptive students from their classrooms, even temporarily. Teachers also usually had almost no influence over the rules surrounding student expulsion from schools. In other words, teachers rarely have the right to not teach particular students, even if they are disruptive and do not wish to be in school. As described by Lortie (1975), the relationship between teacher and student continues to be one of 'dual captivity'; teachers are public servants who cannot choose to not serve their clients and their clients are recipients of a public service who cannot choose to not be served. This stands in sharp distinction to members of the traditional professions, such as lawyers, academics, engineers, accountants, physicians or psychotherapists, who often have a substantial degree of choice over whom they serve and may have the option to not work with particular clients.

This high degree of centralization within schools does not appear to have diminished over the past few decades, and comparing the data in Figure 3 for the early 1990s with that in Figure 4 for 2011–2012, suggests that it may have even increased.[6] For most of the decisions, the percentage of principals reported to have a great deal of influence increased over time. For instance, Figure 4 shows the per cent of principals with high power over curriculum increased from 26% in the 1990's to 49% in 2012. In contrast for many of the decisions, there was a decrease in the per cent of empowered faculties during this same period. This increase the centralization of power within the school could, of course, be an intended consequence of teacher and school accountability pressures.

What is the balance between teachers' responsibility and teachers' control?

From the perspective of the sociology of organizations, occupations and work, the role of teachers in schools can be seen as akin to men or women in the middle (Burawoy, 1979; Edwards, 1979; Perrow, 1986). A useful analogy is that of lower-level supervisors, such as foremen or forewomen, caught between the contradictory demands and needs of their superiors, school administrators, and their subordinates, students (Kanter, 1977; Whyte & Gardner, 1945). In this analogy, teachers are not typically part of the management of schools, nor are teachers the workers. Teachers are in charge of, and responsible for, the workers— their students. While teachers have limited input into crucial school management decisions and decisions concerning their work (as illustrated in Figures 2–4), teachers are delegated a great deal of responsibility for implementing these decisions within their classrooms. Like middlemen and -women in other occupations, teachers usually work alone and may have much responsibility in seeing that their students carry out the tasks assigned to them. This middleman or woman role of teachers within their classrooms may seem similar to professional-like autonomy, but in reality, teachers' classroom practices are highly constrained by larger school-wide decisions, over which teachers have little control or influence. While the work of teachers involves the delegation of much responsibility, our research has documented that it involves little real power.

In considering teachers' role in schools, it is useful to recognize that the motives, values and aspirations of those entering teaching dramatically differ from those entering many other occupations. An unusually large proportion of teachers are motivated by what is called an 'altruistic' or 'public service' ethic. Such individuals place less importance on extrinsic rewards (such as income and prestige) and less emphasis on intrinsic rewards (such as

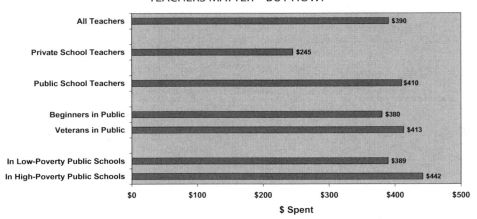

Figure 5. Teachers' responses to: 'in the last school year (2010–2011), how much of your own money did you spend on classroom supplies, without reimbursement'. Data source: 2011–2012 Schools and Staffing Survey.

intellectual challenge or self-expression) and more importance on the opportunity to contribute to the betterment of society, to work with people, to help others, in short, to do 'good.' Numerous studies over past decades have concluded that those entering teaching are more likely to value service and less likely to value pecuniary rewards than are those entering most other occupations, including law, engineering, natural or social science, sales, business, architecture, journalism or art (Bartlett, 2004; Farkas, Johnson, & Foleno, 2000; Lortie, 1975; Miech & Elder, 1996; Roberts, 2013; Rosenberg, 1980).

This altruistic ethic, combined with teachers' mixed role of great responsibility along with little power, is reflected in the widespread practice among teachers of spending their own money on classroom materials. Teachers often find that their school does not, or will not, provide the curriculum materials and supplies they deem necessary to do an adequate job with their students. As illustrated in Figures 3 and 4, the national data show that teachers have little access to, or control over, school budgets and discretionary funds. They must request these monies through the school's administration, a sometimes frustrating and unsuccessful experience. As a result, teachers commonly pay for such materials out of their personal funds.

Since the late 1980s, there have been over a half dozen different national surveys documenting this 'out-of-pocket' spending phenomenon. For example, our analyses of SASS data from the 2011–2012 school year show that teachers spent, on average, about $390 of their own money during the prior year for classroom supplies, without reimbursement (see Figure 5),[7] and only 7% of teachers reported spending none of their own money. Notably, this commitment and public service was not merely a matter of youthful idealism; the data show that older and veteran teachers spent more of their own money, on average, than did younger and beginning teachers. Moreover, public school teachers spent more than did private school teachers, and teachers employed in high-poverty schools spent more than those in low-poverty schools.

Our interpretation of these data on teachers' out-of-pocket expenditures is that they illustrate a remarkable level of responsibility, commitment and a kind of personal accountability, on the part of individuals, even though the organizations that employ these

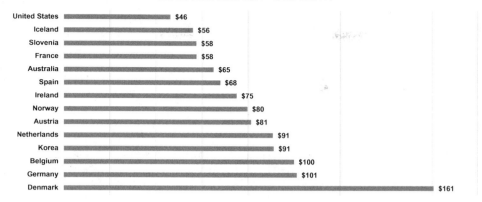

Figure 6. Average public upper-secondary school teacher salary per teaching hour, after 15 years of experience, by nation, 2011 (in 2011 US dollars using purchasing power parities—PPP). Data source: OECD (2014).

individuals offer them little influence and voice into the larger decisions that shape their jobs. The data suggest that in the year 2012 alone, the workforce of 4 million teachers donated over $1.5 billion of educational materials to schools.

Teacher financial subsidization of public schools is especially notable because teaching is a relatively low-paying occupation in the USA. OECD data indicate that teacher salaries in the USA are low compared to those in many other nations (see Figure 6),[8] and SASS data indicate that the average maximum salary possible at the end of one's career was only $65,100 in 2011–2012. Comparing salaries of college graduates within the USA, the average salary (one year after graduation) for college graduates who become teachers is almost 50% less than the average starting salary of classmates who take computer science jobs (Ingersoll & Merrill, 2011). Moreover, this disparity remains throughout the career span. Data from the US Bureau of Labor Statistics (BLS) show that in 2014, the average annual earnings of teachers were less than one-third of the average annual salaries of surgeons, less than one-half those of lawyers, and about two-thirds those of college and university professors in the arts and sciences.

In sum, our argument is that the occupation of teaching in the USA is characterized by an imbalance between responsibilities and power. It is widely recognized that the work of teachers—helping prepare, instruct and rear the next generation of children—is important and consequential. However, those who are entrusted with the training of this next generation—teachers—are not entrusted with much control over many key decisions central to this crucial work. Interestingly, and in contrast to many nations, the education system in the USA is relatively decentralized, with a relatively large share of the decisions surrounding this important work of teachers made at the level of local school districts and schools. However, also in contrast to many other nations, schools themselves are relatively centralized; that is, a relatively small share of the key decisions surrounding the work of teachers is made by teachers themselves. Nevertheless, while teachers are allowed only limited input into these crucial decisions, teachers are delegated a large degree of responsibility for the implementation and success of these decisions. And, teachers appear to have accepted this high degree of responsibility—as evidenced by their high frequency of spending their own money on the needs of the nations's students. Furthermore, this imbalance between responsibilities and power may be increasing. By definition, the objective of the teacher accountability movement has been to hold teachers increasingly responsible for the learning and growth of students. Along with this increased responsibility, however, the trend data shown in Figures 3 and 4 suggest that there has been a decrease in teachers' control over their work and their schools.

What difference does teacher control make?

What difference does the amount of teacher control over their work make for how well schools function? What effect does the amount of teacher influence and control have on life inside schools?

Often, studies assessing the impact of school characteristics focus on student achievement test scores as the primary outcome. In our research, we focused on several non-academic, school climate and teacher stability outcomes: the degree of student misbehaviour, the amount of collegiality and cooperation among teachers and administrators, and teacher retention or turnover in schools. From a sociological perspective and the public's viewpoint a safe, stable and harmonious climate in schools is as important as academic achievement. From much of the public's viewpoint the 'effective' school is characterized by well-behaved students; a collegial, committed staff; and a general sense of cooperation, communication and community. Conversely, the 'ineffective' school is characterized by conflict, distrust and turmoil between students, teachers and administrators (for classic discussions of the importance of the social and non-academic goals of schools and of school climate as an important outcome of schools, see e.g. Coleman, 1987; Dewey, 1974; Durkheim, 1925/1961; Grant, 1988).

Moreover, from an organizational perspective, teacher retention is an important outcome. Some departure of teachers from schools is, of course, normal, inevitable and even beneficial. Some teachers leave classroom teaching to pursue administrative positions or other education-related roles. Others leave the classroom because they discover that teaching is not right for them. Some turnover is due to the termination of low-performing teachers. Nevertheless, it is important to recognize that regardless of the reason, none of these departures are cost-free. All teachers who depart leave a space behind, which takes time and effort to refill.

Elementary and secondary teaching has long been marked by relatively high rates of annual turnover. Analysing national data, we have found that attrition of teachers is similar to that of police officers, higher than nurses and far higher than lawyers, engineers, pharmacists and academics. We have also documented large school-to-school differences in teacher turnover (Ingersoll & Perda, in press). Finally, we have documented that teacher turnover is the major factor behind teacher shortages, particularly in math and science (Ingersoll, 2001; Ingersoll & Perda, 2010) and that working conditions and leadership actions affect teacher turnover (Ingersoll & May, 2012). The data make it clear that to ensure students are taught by qualified teachers, schools must improve teacher retention.

To evaluate the relationship between the amount of control and power held by teachers and these kinds of outcomes, we undertook a series of advanced multilevel regression analyses of the SASS data (Ingersoll, 2003). In these analyses, we controlled for the effects of other school characteristics, such as school size; student poverty levels; whether a school is

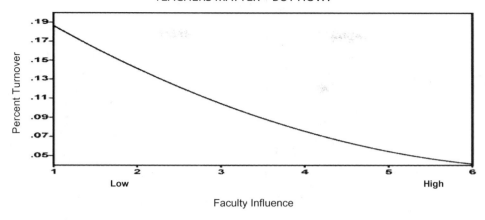

Figure 7. Per cent annual voluntary turnover of teachers, by amount of faculty influence in the school over student discipline policies. Source: Ingersoll (2003).

in an urban, rural or suburban setting; and whether it is private or public and also for other teacher characteristics, such as experience, fields, gender and race.

Our analyses found that, while most schools are centralized, there is substantial variation among schools in the degree of teacher control among different kinds of schools and the latter is strongly linked to how well schools function. Schools where teachers have more control over key school-wide and classroom decisions have fewer problems with student misbehaviour, have more collegiality and cooperation among teachers and administrators and retain more of their teachers.

However, we also found that the magnitude of these effects of teacher control and influence on outcomes is dependent on the type of decision or issue involved. Interestingly, the data show that one of the most consequential sets of decisions has to do with a particular group of social and nonacademic issues—school and classroom student behaviour and discipline policies. We found a strong relationship between the average amount of teacher influence over discipline decisions and the likelihood that teachers stay in, or voluntarily depart from, their schools. As shown in Figure 7, almost 1 in 5 teachers in schools with a low level of teacher control over student discipline issues was likely to depart from their schools, while far fewer, less than 1 in 20, was likely to do so from schools with a high level of teacher control over such issues.[9]

Why is teacher control over this particular set of social and nonacademic issues so consequential? Our research has indicated that this issue is characterized by significant imbalance between teachers' responsibilities and teachers' control. Teachers are responsible for enforcing student rules and maintaining an orderly classroom. But the SASS data tell us that teachers often have little input into the rules, norms and standards for students; these policies are largely conceived by others. In our field work, we found that teachers often have little say over the types of sanctions used to enforce the rules. Many teachers are not allowed to remove students who are disrupting their classrooms, must first obtain permission to sanction a student infraction and cannot punish students caught cheating on tests. These limitations on teacher control can undermine their ability to take charge of their classrooms and to meet their job responsibilities. And, our statistical analyses indicate that this lack of control is related to high teacher turnover rates.

TEACHERS MATTER – BUT HOW?

From our perspective, at the crux of successful teaching is the level of control and power teachers have on issues for which they are responsible. If teachers have sufficient say over the decisions surrounding activities for which they are responsible, they will be more able to ensure the job is done properly and, in turn, derive respect from administrators, colleagues and students. On the other hand, if teachers' power and control over school and classroom policies is not sufficient to accomplish the tasks for which they are responsible, they will meet neither group's needs and will sour their relationships. The teacher who has little control and power is the teacher who is less able to get things done is the teacher with less credibility. Students can more easily ignore such a teacher; indeed, timidity seems to invite challenge. Principals can more easily neglect backing them. Peers may be more likely to shun them. This, in turn, could lead such teachers to feel less commitment to their teaching job or the teaching career.

The importance of balance between teachers' responsibilities and power was further born out in a separate study we conducted using SASS/TFS data, on the impact of accountability reforms on teacher retention (Ingersoll et al., 2016; Ingersoll et al., in press). Our primary focus was on school-level accountability reforms and not individual teacher accountability mechanisms. We examined whether each of the typical steps (see Figure 1) involved in school accountability—the setting of standards for school performance, the use of state or district assessments to measure performance, how well the school performed in regard to the standards and the application of any subsequent incentives or sanctions at the school level—had an association with the subsequent turnover of teachers from those schools.

Our advanced multilevel regression analyses of the SASS/TFS data showed that after controlling for the background characteristics of teachers and schools, some steps in school accountability reforms had an association with teacher turnover and some did not. Having standards and assessments in schools themselves did not have an association with teacher retention. In contrast, school performance did matter; lower-performing schools had far higher turnover than higher-performing schools. Rewards given to higher-performing schools did little to improve the already higher retention, but sanctions applied to lower-performing schools were related to increases in their already higher turnover.

Though sanctions are associated with increased turnover, our analyses revealed that teacher attrition is not inevitable at sanctioned lower-performing schools. Following our sociology of organizations, occupations and work perspective, we examined the role of school organizational conditions in the relationship between school accountability and teacher turnover, since state-mandated accountability policies do not necessarily mandate specific corrective methods (Fuhrman & Elmore, 2004; Smith & O'Day, 1990). We analysed the interaction of accountability reforms and a selection of working and organizational conditions long associated with the effectiveness of schools—the quality of school leadership, the amount of classroom resources and support provided to teachers, the level of school-wide faculty influence over decision-making and the degree of autonomy teachers have in their classrooms—in the context of teacher turnover. Indeed, positive conditions do ameliorate the effects of sanctions in low-performing schools. In particular, one variable stood out—how much autonomy teachers were allowed in their own classrooms over key issues such as selecting textbooks and other instructional materials, selecting content, topics and skills to be taught, selecting teaching techniques, evaluating and grading students, determining the amount of homework to be assigned and disciplining students. The data

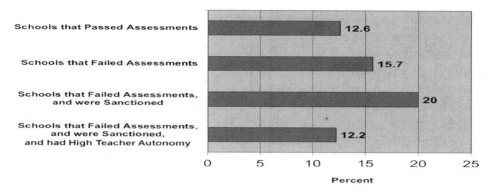

Figure 8. Predicted probabilities of teacher turnover, by school performance, sanctions and level of teacher autonomy, 2004–2005. Source: Ingersoll et al. (2016).

showed that low-performing schools with sanctions had far lower turnover if their teachers were allowed more autonomy in their own classrooms.

Figure 8 illustrates the differences we found in the probability of teacher turnover, according to school performance, sanctions and teacher autonomy. On average, 12.6% of the teachers in the higher-performing schools departed between the 2004 and 2005 school years. Turnover was significantly higher—20%—in those lower-performing schools that had been subsequently sanctioned. However, those lower-performing sanctioned schools which allowed teachers greater classroom autonomy had significantly lower turnover—and at a rate (12.2%) similar to that in higher-performing schools.[10] These findings suggest that there is an important role for the leadership, management and organizational conditions in these schools.

Conclusion

The importance of teacher accountability has become a growing part of the conventional wisdom about what ails teaching and has had an increasing impact on reform and policy. Our view is that proponents of the accountability reforms identify important issues and problems. Accountability in schools is reasonable and necessary, and the public has a right and, indeed, an obligation to be concerned with the performance of teachers.

Our argument, however, is that the teacher accountability perspective offers only a partial, one-sided explanation. As a result, it often overlooks the ways schools themselves, in particular how they are managed, contribute to the teacher quality problem. The data show that the high degree of centralization in schools and a lack of teacher control, rather than the opposite, is often the source of problems in low-functioning schools. As a result, top-down accountability reforms may divert attention from the organizational sources of school problems.

Additionally, proponents of top-down accountability reforms often overlook the unusual character of the teaching workforce. Common among these analysts and reformers is a teacher-deficit viewpoint, assuming that blame lies with the calibre of individual teachers. But the data suggest that teachers have an unusual degree of public service orientation and commitment, compared with many other occupations. Unrecognized and unappreciated by these critics is the extent to which the teaching workforce is a source of human, social and even financial capital in schools.

Finally, for the preceding reasons, teacher accountability reforms often do not work well. Top-down reforms draw attention to an important set of needs—accountability on the part of those doing the work. But these kinds of reforms sometimes overlook another equally important set of needs—the autonomy and engagement of those doing the work. Too much organizational control may deny teachers the very control and flexibility they need to do the job effectively and undermine the motivation of those doing the job. A high degree of centralized control may squander a valuable human resource—the unusual degree of commitment of those who enter the teaching occupation. Having little control over the terms, processes and outcomes of their work may undermine the ability of teachers to feel they are doing worthwhile work, the very reason many of them came into the occupation in the first place, and end up contributing to the high rates of turnover among teachers. As a result, such centralizing reforms may not only fail to solve the problems they seek to address but also end up making things worse. In plain terms, simply recruiting quality candidates and holding them more accountable will not solve the problem of quality if the manner in which the job itself is organized and managed undermines those same candidates.

A prominent line of thought in the sociology of organizations, occupations and work and in the practical realm of organizational leadership (e.g. Drucker, 1973, 1992; Whyte & Blasi, 1982) advocates a balanced approach to implementing accountability in work settings. In this view, organizational accountability and employee control must go hand in hand in workplaces, and increases in one must be accompanied by increases in the other; imbalances between the two can result in problems for both employees and for organizations. Delegating autonomy or control to employees without also ensuring commensurate accountability can foster inefficiencies and irresponsible behaviour and lead to low performance. Likewise, administering organizational accountability without providing commensurate autonomy to employees can foster job dissatisfaction, increase employee turnover and lead to low performance. Translating this management perspective for the case of schools suggests that it does not make sense to hold teachers accountable for issues they do not control, nor does it make sense to give teachers control over issues for which they are not held accountable. Both of these changes are necessary, and neither alone is sufficient.

From a sociology of organizations, occupations and work perspective, this balanced approach is a key characteristic underlying the model of the established professions—law, medicine, university professors, engineering, in particular (Freidson, 1986; Hodson & Sullivan, 1995). Professional work involves highly complex sets of skills, intellectual functioning and knowledge that are not easily acquired and not widely held. For this reason, professions are often referred to as 'knowledge-based' occupations. In the professional model, practitioners are, ideally, first provided with the training, resources, conditions and autonomy to do the job and then held accountable for doing the job well.

Promising examples of a more balanced and professional-like model of school organization have sprung up in recent years in the USA. For example, there is a growing network of schools that are operated and run by teachers (Kolderie, 2008, 2014). These schools are often referred to as 'partnership schools' because they are modelled after law partnerships, where lawyers both manage, and ultimately are accountable for, the organization and its success (Hawkins, 2009).

TEACHERS MATTER – BUT HOW?

From our sociology of organizations, occupations and work perspective, solving the problem of teacher quality will require addressing the underlying roots of the problem. In contrast to a teacher-deficit perspective, the focus of reform should shift from solely attracting or developing 'better people for the job' to also securing 'a better job for the people' (Kolderie, 2008). Rather than forcing the existing arrangement to work better, this alternative perspective suggests the importance of also viewing teacher quality issues as organizational and occupational design issues, implying the need for a different arrangement, better built for those who do the work of teaching.

Notes

1. The International Survey of the Locus of Decision-Making in Educational Systems was part of the INES of the Center for Educational Research and Innovation of the OECD in 1990–1991 and 1997–1998. Later a similar version of this survey was incorporated into PISA. The data in Figure 2 were collected from public elementary and secondary schools by PISA in 2012 with principals assessing responsibility for tasks such as hiring teachers and determining course content. In Figure 2, the estimates refer to the percentages of principal/respondents that reported a group or level had considerable responsibility, adjusted if respondents reported more than one group/level had responsibility. For example, if a principal reported that they were the only group/level with considerable responsibility, we allocated 1.0 to them for that question, but if the principal reported they, the school board and teachers all had considerable responsibility, we allocated 0.33 to each, and so on. We then summed the points per group and divided by the total for each nation to calculate each group/level's per cent. For further information on the 1990–1991 survey, see Organisation for Economic Co-operation and Development (OECD, 1995). For details on the 1997–1998 survey, see OECD (1998). For further information on the 2012 PISA survey, see OECD (2013).
2. See, for example, Perrow (1986), Edwards (1979), Burawoy (1979), Frey (1971), and Lukes (1974).
3. The data in Figure 3 on discipline, hiring and curriculum are from the school administrator questionnaire of the 1990–1991 SASS. The sample size was 4110 secondary schools. The data on the budget, teacher evaluation and inservice are from the school administrator questionnaire of the 1993–1994 SASS. The sample size was 4031 secondary schools. In SASS, principals at each school were asked to rate the influence of school boards, principals and teachers at their school on several activities. In the 1993–1994 questionnaire, school district staff were also included as a group and are counted here with school boards. The questions used a six-point scale from one = 'none' to six = 'a great deal.' In Figure 3, we defined the groups as having a 'great deal of influence' if their score was six on the scale. The data on teacher assignment and student tracking in Figure 3 are from the 1993 NCES Survey of High School Curricular Options (SHSCO). This survey was a supplement based on a public school subset of the 1990–1991 SASS. Like the SASS administrator questionnaire, the SHSCO also asked principals about the influence of different groups on several school decisions, but the questionnaires differed slightly in wording and scale. The SHSCO questions used a four-point scale from 'not at all' to 'a great extent.' In Figure 3, we defined the groups as having a 'great deal of influence' if their score was four on the scale. The sample size was 912 public secondary schools. For the item on student tracking, the groups evaluated were school governing boards, school principals and teacher department heads (not teachers). For the item on teacher assignment, the groups evaluated were school district administrators, school principals and teachers. Because these data were not collected for private schools and also not available for disaggregation, they are not included. For more details on these analyses, see Ingersoll (2003).
4. The data in Figure 4 are from the school administrator and the teacher questionnaires of the 2011–2012 SASS. The sample size was 11,000 secondary schools. In the 2011–2012 SASS, principals and teachers at each school were asked to assess their own influence on various aspects of school policy, such as establishing curriculum and setting discipline policy. The

TEACHERS MATTER – BUT HOW?

questions used a four-point scale from one = 'none' to four = 'a great deal'. In Figure 4, we defined the groups as having a 'great deal of influence' if their score was four on the scale.

5. For discussion of the case of higher education, see, for example, Mills (1951), Krause (1971), Clark (1987), or Grant and Murray (1999).

6. The apparent changes over time in the percentage of empowered faculties must be interpreted with caution. Across the SASS surveys, those asked about the distribution of power changed. In the earlier SASS surveys, principals were the respondents reporting on both their influence and that of faculties in their schools. However, in 2012, principals only reported on their own level of influence, while teachers were asked to report on the influence of faculties in their schools. Hence, it is unclear if the apparent decreases in faculty empowerment are real or are a result of a change in respondents.

7. The data in Figure 5 are from the 2011–2012 SASS.

8. The data in Figure 6 are from the OECD's *Education at a glance 2014: OECD indicators*. Retrieved from http://www.oecd-ilibrary.org/education/education-at-a-glance-2014_eag-2014-en. PPP refers to purchasing power parity and is a measure used to standardize salaries, in US dollars, by taking into account the relative purchasing power for private consumption and the standard of living in different nations. Gross teachers' salaries were converted using PPPs for private consumption from OECD National Accounts. The period of reference for teachers' salaries is from 1 July 2011 to 30 June 2012. The reference date for PPPs is 2011–2012. The data on teachers' salaries were collected by the 2013 OECD-INES Survey on Teachers and the Curriculum.

9. The data analysed in Figure 7 are from the 1991–1992 TFS. The analysis was based on a sample of 6733 teachers from 4864 schools. See the Appendix of Ingersoll (2003) for detailed information on the sample, measures, methods utilized. Note that in order to focus on those kinds of departures that were more likely to be related to the character of schools, the analysis excluded teachers who departed their jobs because of retirement, lay-offs or school closings or because of being fired or terminated.

10. The data analysed in Figure 8 are for public schools and from the 2003–2004 SASS and 2004–2005 TFS. In the middle of the 2003–2004 school year, SASS asked a national sample of school-level administrators if, in the prior school year (2002–2003), their school had been subject to school performance standards established by their district or state, whether their school had been subject to evaluations assessing their performance in regard to the standards, and how their school fared on the assessments. These administrators were then asked whether their school subsequently, in the current 2003–2004 school year, received rewards, incentives, penalties or sanctions as a result of the school's performance. Subsequently, the TFS obtained data on which teachers, from the original 2003–2004 SASS teacher sample, stayed in, or departed from, their schools, or from teaching altogether, by the following year—2004–2005. Hence, the 2003–2005 SASS/TFS provides a clear timeline of the steps in accountability (see Figure 1): schools' standards set and performance assessed in 2002–2003; rewards or sanctions subsequently applied to schools in 2003–2004; teacher retention or turnover between 2003–2004 and 2004–2005. In our analysis, we used logistic regression to examine the relationship between each of the steps of school accountability and the likelihood that individual teachers depart from their schools, while controlling for individual-level characteristics of teachers and school demographic characteristics. In the regression models, the dependent variable—teacher turnover—was based on whether each teacher remained with his or her school ('stayers'), or departed from his or her school in the year subsequent to the administration of the accountability steps. The latter outcome includes both those who left teaching altogether ('leavers') and those who moved between schools ('movers'). For more detail on the data and methods utilized in the analyses, see Ingersoll et al. (in press).

Disclosure statement

No potential conflict of interest was reported by the authors.

References

Bartlett, L. (2004). Expanding teacher work roles: A resource for retention or a recipe for overwork? *Journal of Education Policy, 19*, 565–582.

Bennett, W. (1993). *The book of virtues.* New York, NY: Simon & Schuster.

Burawoy, M. (1979). *Manufacturing consent: Changes in the labor process under monopoly capitalism.* Chicago, IL: University of Chicago Press.

Clark, B. (1987). *The academic life: Small worlds, different worlds.* New York, NY: Carnegie Foundation for the Advancement of Teaching.

Coleman, J. (1987). Families and schools. *Educational Researcher, 16*, 32–38.

Dewey, J. (1902/1974). *The child and the curriculum.* Chicago, IL: University of Chicago Press.

Drucker, P. (1973). *Management: Tasks, responsibilities, practices.* New York, NY: Harper & Row.

Drucker, P. (1992). *Managing for the future: The 1990s and beyond.* New York, NY: Truman Talley.

Durkheim, E. (1925/1961). *Moral education: A study in the theory and application of the sociology of education.* (E. K. Wilson & H. Schnurer, Trans.). New York, NY: Free Press.

Edwards, R. (1979). *Contested terrain.* New York, NY: Basic Books.

Elmore, R. (2000). *Building a new structure for school leadership.* New York, NY: Albert Shanker Institute.

Farkas, S., Johnson, J., & Foleno, T. (2000). *A sense of calling: Who teaches and why.* New York, NY: Public Agenda.

Finn, C., Kanstoroom, M., & Petrilli, M. (1999). *The quest for better teachers: Grading the states.* Washington, DC: Thomas B. Fordham Foundation.

Freidson, E. (1986). *Professional powers: A study in the institutionalization of formal knowledge.* Chicago, IL: University of Chicago Press.

Frey, F. (1971). On issues and non-issues in the study of power. *American Political Science Review, 65*, 1091–1104.

Fuhrman, S., & Elmore, R. (Eds.). (2004). *Redesigning accountability systems for education* (pp. 189–219). New York, NY: Teachers College Press.

Goldring, R., Gray, L., & Bitterman, A. (2013). *Characteristics of public and private elementary and secondary school teachers in the United States: Results from the 2011–12 Schools and Staffing Survey* (NCES 2013-314). Washington, DC: National Center for Education Statistics, U.S. Department of Education. Retrieved from http://nces.ed.gov/pubsearc

Goldstein, D. (2015). *The teacher wars.* New York: Anchor Books.

Graham, S., Parmer, R., Chambers, L., Tourkin, S., & Lyter, D. (2011). *Documentation for the 2008–09 Teacher Follow-up Survey* (NCES 2011-304). Washington, DC: National Center for Education Statistics, U.S. Department of Education. Retrieved from http://nces.ed.gov/pubsearch

Grant, G. (1988). *The world we created at Hamilton high.* Cambridge, MA: Harvard University Press.

Grant, G., & Murray, C. (1999). *Teaching in America: The slow revolution.* Cambridge, MA: Harvard University Press.

Hawkins, B. (2009). Teacher cooperatives: What happens when teachers run the school? *Education Next, 9*, 37–41.

Hershberg, T. (2005). Value-added assessment and systemic reform: A response to the challenge of human capital development. *Phi Delta Kappan, 87*, 276–283.

Hodson, R., & Sullivan, T. (1995). Professions and professionals. In *The social organization of work* (pp. 287–314). Belmont, CA: Wadsworth.

TEACHERS MATTER – BUT HOW?

Ingersoll, R. (1999). The problem of underqualified teachers in American secondary schools. *Educational Researcher, 28*, 26–37.

Ingersoll, R. (2001). Teacher turnover and teacher shortages: An organizational analysis. *American Educational Research Journal, 38*, 499–534.

Ingersoll, R. (2003). *Who controls teachers' work? Power and accountability in America's schools.* Cambridge, MA: Harvard University Press.

Ingersoll, R. (2004). Why some schools have more underqualified teachers than others. In D. Ravitch (Ed.), *Brookings Papers on Education Policy* (pp. 45–71). Washington, DC: Brookings Institution.

Ingersoll, R. (2012). Power, accountability and the teacher quality problem. In S. Kelly (Ed.), *Assessing teacher quality: Understanding teacher effects on instruction and achievement* (Chapter 5, pp. 97–109). New York, NY: Teachers' College Press.

Ingersoll, R., & May, H. (2012). The magnitude, destinations and determinants of mathematics and science teacher turnover. Co-authored with H. May. *Educational Evaluation and Policy Analysis, 34*, 435–464.

Ingersoll, R., & Merrill, E. (2011). The status of teaching as a profession. In J. Ballantine & J. Spade (Eds.), *Schools and society: A sociological perspective* (4th ed., pp. 185–198). Belmont, CA: Wadsworth Press.

Ingersoll, R., Merrill, E., & May, H. (2016, May). Do accountability policies push teachers out? *Educational Leadership, 73*, 44–49.

Ingersoll, R., Merrill, E., & May, H. (in press). *What are the effects of school accountability on teacher turnover?* (CPRE Research Report). Consortium for Policy Research in Education, University of Pennsylvania.

Ingersoll, R., & Perda, D. (2010). Is the supply of mathematics and science teachers sufficient? *American Educational Research Journal, 47*, 563–594.

Ingersoll, R., & Perda, D. (in press). *How high is teacher turnover and is it a problem?* Philadelphia: Consortium for Policy Research in Education, University of Pennsylvania.

Kanter, R. (1977). *Men and women of the corporation.* New York, NY: Basic Books.

Kirst, M. (1984). *Who controls our schools? American values in conflict.* New York, NY: W. H. Freeman.

Kolderie, T. (2008). *The other half of the strategy: Following up on systemic reform by innovating with school and schooling.* St Paul, MN: Education Evolving.

Kolderie, T. (2014). *The split screen strategy: How to turn education into a self-improving system.* Edina, MN: Beaver's Pond Press.

Krause, E. (1971). *The sociology of occupations.* Boston, MA: Little-Brown.

Levin, H. (1998). Educational performance standards and the economy. *Educational Researcher, 27*, 4–10.

Lortie, D. (1975). *School teacher.* Chicago, IL: University of Chicago Press.

Lukes, S. (1974). *Power: A radical view.* London: Macmillan.

Miech, R., & Elder, G. (1996). The service ethic and teaching. *Sociology of Education, 69*, 237–253.

Mills, C. W. (1951). *White collar.* New York, NY: Oxford University Press.

Moulthrop, D., Calegari, N., & Eggers, D. (2005). *Teachers have it easy: The big sacrifices and small salaries of America's teachers.* New York City: The New Press.

National Center for Education Statistics. (2011–2013). *Schools and Staffing Survey (SASS) and Teacher Followup Survey (TFS).* Washington, DC: U.S. Department of Education.

National Council on Teacher Quality. (2010). *Teacher layoffs: Rethinking "last hired, first fired" policies.* Washington, DC: Author. Retrieved from http://www.nctq.org/p/docs/nctq_dc_layoffs.pdf

New Teacher Project. (2010). *A smarter teacher layoff system: How quality-based layoffs can help schools keep great teachers in tough economic times.* Brooklyn, NY: Author. Retrieved from http://www.tntp.org/files/TNTP_Smarter_Teacher_Layoffs_Mar10.pdf

Organisation for Economic Co-operation and Development. (1995). *Decision-making in 14 OECD education systems.* Paris: Author.

Organisation for Economic Co-operation and Development. (1998). *Education at a glance: OECD indicators.* Paris: Author.

Organisation for Economic Co-operation and Development. (2013). *PISA 2012 results: What makes schools successful? Resources, policies and practices* (Vol. IV). Paris: Author.

Organisation for Economic Co-operation and Development. (2014). *Education at a glance 2014: OECD indicators.* Paris: Author. http://dx.doi.org/10.1787/eag-2014-en

Perrow, C. (1986). *Complex organizations: A critical essay*. New York, NY: Random.

Roberts, S. (2013). Incentives, teachers and gender at work. *Education Policy Analysis Archives, 21*(31), 1–25.

Rosenberg, M. (1980). *Occupations and values*. New York, NY: Arno Press.

Sadker, M., & Sadker, D. (1994). *Failing at fairness*. New York, NY: Scribner.

Santoro, D. (2011). Good teaching in difficult times: Demoralization in the pursuit of good work. *American Journal of Education, 118*(1), 1–23.

Smith, M., & O'Day, J. (1990). Systemic school reform. In S. Fuhrman & B. Malen (Eds.), *Politics of education yearbook 1990* (pp. 133–267). New York, NY: Taylor and Francis.

Thomas, E., & Wingert, P. (2010, March 6). Why we must fire bad teachers. *Newsweek*.

Tyack, D. (1974). *The one best system*. Cambridge, MA: Harvard University Press.

United States Bureau of Labor Statistics. (2014, May). *National occupational employment and wage estimates*. Washington, DC: Author.

Urban League. (1999). *The state of Black America*. New York, NY: Urban League.

Whyte, W. F., & Blasi, J. (1982). Worker ownership, participation, and control: Toward a theoretical model. *Policy Sciences, 14*, 137–163.

Whyte, W. F., & Gardner, B. (1945). The man in the middle. *Applied Anthropology, 4*, 1–28.

Enacted realities in teachers' experiences: bringing materialism into pragmatism

Elin Sundström Sjödin and Ninni Wahlström

ABSTRACT

In this article we explore factors that constitute 'the social' for the teacher Susan, which at the same time highlights ethical aspects of the exercise of her profession. We meet her in a situation where she is setting grades, and our interest focuses on the relations that become of concern for her in her professional task to give the students their grades. In this exploration, we recognize the renewal of interest in realism and examine the possible links that can be drawn between transactional realism, as a pragmatic view, and the new materialism, here represented by actor–network theory. Building on a narrative from an interview with a named teacher in a daily newspaper, the empirical study focuses on actors constituting Susan's reality when grading. Our argument is that in order to understand the complex levels of aspects that influence teachers' actions, it is necessary to start from the local and from there trace the human and material factors that may affect teachers' room for action. Bringing material aspects into the consideration of Susan's situation helps us see that technology itself changes time and spaces and moves the action of grading into spaces outside her professional sphere.

In this study we explore how teachers in their profession are influenced by external pressure from human and non-human sources, challenging the moral and ethical aspects of the exercise of their profession. The study illustrates how teachers matter in an ongoing shift from an epistemological form of professional accountability, associated with notions of truth and objectivity shared between those knowledgeable within a subject, and an administrative form of accountability, linked to more generic skills in terms of competencies in a school subject (Young, 2008).

In recent years, there has been a renaissance of interest in pragmatism's relevance to social science and a revivification of interest in pragmatist philosophy among social scientists. In terms of a 'post-postmodern[1]' approach, this renewed interest in pragmatism revolves around two turns. The first is the realist version of reflexivity inherent in pragmatic philosophy. The second concerns the temporal frame of social inquiry that places reflexive realism in a future-oriented ontology in terms of possible consequences of inquiries. These turns are in line with contemporary theories collectively referred to as the new materialism (Rosiek,

2013). This renewed interest in the realist aspect of pragmatism should be viewed against the backdrop of a wider philosophical discussion between the realist and constructivist positions on gaining knowledge of the world. For example, Ferraris (2014) suggests in a manifesto that the time has come for a 'new realism'. He argues that realism and construc-tionism have different validity areas and that each position has equal legitimacy within its area. In this article, we recognize the renewal of interest in realism and examine the possible correlations that can be drawn between the aforementioned 'renewal' of interest in trans-actional realism (cf. Biesta, 2014; Rosiek, 2013) and the 'new materialism', here represented by actor–network theory (ANT). Our argument is that to really understand the different levels of aspects that influence teachers' actions and the condition of teaching, it is necessary to start from the local and from there trace the human and material factors that may affect teachers' actions. Thus, the starting point needs to be taken from areas of space and time where teachers are actually affected in their work, whether inside or outside the institution of school.

Purpose and research question

The purpose of this study is to contribute to the contemporary discussion of a realist per-spective in curriculum research. However, instead of understanding the material structure as superior to the social, as in critical realism (Bhaskar, 1997), or understanding knowledge as context-independent, as in social realism (Moore & Young, 2010; Wheelahan, 2010; Young, 2008), we examine how temporality in transactional realism can facilitate a more complete understanding of factors within and outside the institutional environment of school that form different but overlapping networks for teachers, potentially affecting their room for action.

In the first part of the article, we explore the notion of 'transactional realism' in Dewey's pragmatism and examine the possible links between the 'provisional' in a pragmatic view of realism and the potentiality of 'the social', comprising both social and material factors, in ANT. In the second part of the article, we investigate an authentic teacher narrative concern-ing a teacher's experience of grading students to demonstrate how an approach to materi-alism can contribute to a broader understanding of factors that can potentially affect a teacher's experience of room for action. In the third and final part, we discuss the implication of combining pragmatism with materialism to capture the situations that affect teachers' work in a way that is not usually paid attention to.

The research questions explored in this stydy are: How can we understand 'the social' as a temporal assemblage of material and non-material factors? What factors and phenomena are gathered as 'the social' for the teacher in our empirical example?

Enacting realities in practice

Dewey's philosophical naturalism brings with it a particular form of realism. For Dewey, the terms 'change' and 'temporality' are inherited in the concept of 'nature'. All matter is subject to change; therefore, matter is not a substance but a function of natural events involved in a structure of motion. Stable matter is stable because it changes relatively slowly (Westbrook, 1991). Because everything is subject to change and temporality, Dewey's realism is 'provi-sional'. This provisional realism becomes evident in Dewey's construction of the concept of experience. Dewey argued that experience is a relation between a human being and his or her physical and social environment. The term experience comprises an understanding of an objective world 'which enters into the actions and sufferings of men and undergoes modifications through their responses' (Dewey, 1917/1985, p. 6). By its connection with the unknown, experience is experimental and oriented towards the future. Reflection is constantly present in every conscious experience where relations, connections, and the striving to handle situations constitute the meaning of the object. In Dewey's philosophy of logic, 'experience is what logic is all about'; logic is not a matter of a priori principles but rather a matter of a 'theory of inquiry' and a 'theory of existence' that are linked together by a theory of language (Sleeper, 1986/2001, p. 6).

As Westbrook (2005, p. 40) notes, it is a 'piecemeal realism' Dewey argues for, having to do with human actions involved in the process of inquiry. There are things that are existentially real, but they are not real in any essentialist way; instead, they are 'contingently real objects' and not 'permanently real' (Westbrook, 2005, p. 147, *italics in original*). Their characteristics are temporal in two ways: things are contingent in relation to human inquiries, but they are also contingent in relation to the conditions that shaped these things in a special fashion. Therefore, these changing conditions are also temporal and cannot be taken for granted; instead they need to be taken into account when thinking of 'the real' (Sleeper, 1986/2001; Westbrook, 2005).

Dewey's logic of theory and piecemeal realism means that logic 'transforms reality even as reality transforms the logical agent' (Garrison, 1994, pp. 7–8). The transactional understanding of the concept of meaning and experience implies that the 'world' (or environment) is influenced by our actions and vice versa. 'The reality, including the functional structure of a given context, is in the transactions among all those events that participate in the context including the participation of the inquirer' (Garrison, 1994, p. 13). Therefore, 'objectivity' can only be reached by intersubjectivity, that is, by communicating our understanding of the world with others' understanding of the same occurrences and objects (see also Davidson, 1991/2001; Wahlström, 2010). Bernstein (2010) considers the notion of experience a fundamental part of Dewey's philosophy, even after the linguistic turn. Regarding Rorty's (1992) argument that humans' use of linguistic expressions is the key for creating meaning, Bernstein states that a 'linguistic pragmatism', which does not pay attention to the role of experience in the human condition, risks being transformed into a linguistic idealism that underestimates the limitations and the resistance expressed through the experiences in people's daily lives. Each creation of meaning must ultimately be related to human experiencing. Bernstein claims that the challenge for pragmatism after the linguistic turn lies in integrating the concept of experience into an understanding of meaning and knowledge of the world.

Because meaning is reconstructed in relation to the consequences of a phenomenon, the distinction between 'the private' and 'the public' is not a distinction between the individual and the social; instead, it is a difference between who is concerned with the consequences of an actual communicative transaction. When consequences are restricted to the people engaged in conversation, the action is limited to a private network. When the consequences of a communication instead go beyond the people actually involved in conversation, the 'act acquires a public capacity' (Dewey, 1927/1991, p. 13). The point made by Dewey is that actions that are private or public, as well as the character of other human actions, cannot be decided beforehand. The uncertain boundaries between private and public are probably even truer in our time when communication includes digital communication.

According to Latour (2011, p. 11), Dewey 'invented reflexive modernization before the expression was coined'. In line with this line of thought, it is an unreflective faith in rationality that has led to the risks and shortcomings in the industrial society (see Beck & Grande, 2007). There is no safe and stable knowledge from which we, or rather the experts, can act. Instead, we need to handle the occurrences and problems around us as 'a public', that is, in terms of collective experimentation and exploration. In our daily experience, we act without basing our actions on absolute certainty; instead, we try to act with care and caution because we do not know 'for sure' the consequences of our actions related to humans and non-humans. The same is true for the common actions as a public. There is not one nature but 'many competing natures' that need to be kept together in what Latour (2011) terms a common 'collective experiment'. According to Latour (2011, p. 9), the common world is not behind us as 'a solid and disputable ground for agreement, but before us, as a risky and highly disputable goal that remains very far in the future'. It is in this sense Latour finds the Deweyan approach to the concept of the public 'as fresh as in 1927', when Dewey first published the text *The Public and Its Problems*. The public is presented by Dewey as a collection of people pulled together by a shared problem, not necessarily by choice. Members of a public have been 'inducted' into it rather than volunteering for it (Bennett, 2010, p. 101). After the modern era, Latour argues, what we now have to rely on are the inquiries and the reflections of the public. The public 'begins with what we cannot see nor predict, with the unintended, unwanted, invisible consequences of our collective actions' (Latour, 2011, pp. 10–11).

The centrality of becoming

The 'open' and 'uncertain' being central features of Dewey's pragmatism both anticipates and unites pragmatism with philosophical orientations in our own time (e.g. Garrison, 1999; Hickman, 2007; Semetsky, 2006). When the starting point is not taken in an active subject but in the movement that precedes the subject, as in Gilles Deleuze's and Félix Guattari's philosophy, learning is no longer about an active subject learning about passive objects. In a traditional view of knowledge, it is the subject that determines what knowledge is, and in a social constructivist approach, the subject also creates the knowledge. By including materiality and ascribing it agency, the distinction between subject and object is loosened (Johansson, 2015). For Dewey, as for Deleuze, reorganization of experience constitutes 'a continuous process of adaptation and readaptation' in the process of subject formation (Semetsky, 2006, p. 39). In Deleuze's terms, temporality is conceptualized as 'becoming' and in Dewey's terms as 'continuity' and 'transaction'.

Ascribing materiality agency does not mean that all human and non-human actors are of equal importance. Latour states that ANT is not the 'establishment of some absurd 'symmetry between humans and non-humans''. Symmetric only means '*not* to impose a priori some spurious *asymmetry* among human intentional action and a material world of causal relations' (2007, p. 76, *italics in original*). Thus, the term 'symmetric' means that there is not an a priori asymmetric relationship between human actions and the material world.

Accepting a heterogeneous network as performative and as making a difference includes not assuming beforehand what becomes of importance and what makes the biggest difference. It is the transaction between the no-matter-what-kind-of actors that constitutes practice and what becomes real. This turn is made possible through a displacement of focus from matters of fact to matters of concern (Latour 2007). An implication of this turn is that things or material processes that are part of the assemblages, networks, or events, have substantial political performativity, a 'politics of what' (Mol, 2002, p. 172). The purpose of such an approach is to move beyond regarding materials as naturalized artifacts and to recognize its normative and political dimensions. This is the move from objects to things, from matters of fact to matters of concern.

In this article, we do not take 'the social' as a given stable entity. Instead, the social is regarded as temporal connections between things assembled in contingent ways given a certain state of affairs. The teacher's possible agency is linked to the forms of network the teacher encounters in her environment.

> From an ANT perspective, what appears to be the teacher's agency is an effect of different forces, including actions, desires, capacities and connections that move through her, as well as the forces exerted by the texts and technologies in all educational encounters. (Fenwick et al., 2011, p. 112)

Therefore, following this logic, 'the social' is not the beginning but the end of an inquiry. The aim of such inquiry is not to explain something by social factors but to show how the social becomes visible in re-associations and reassembling of associations by tracing how new institutions and processes are able to assemble important social fluids into networks that form 'the social' (Latour, 2007, p. 11). The relations that make up a network are not given and do not last by themselves; rather, the links and nodes in the network need to be supported and maintained by other links and nodes. Consequently, networks are 'processes and achievements rather than relations and structures that are given in the order of things' (Law, 2003, p. 3). This process and achievement of supporting a network needs specific means to produce and maintain the social; in our example, this is the reality of teachers, the spaces enacted by the transactions, and the realities transacted in the spaces. Enactment of phenomena means that they are created in and through relations between a complex and heterogeneous set of actors (Mol, 2002).

What is 'real' is what is taking form and shape through its performance in webs of relations. Just as in Dewey's transactions, objects and subjects are not real in themselves and neither are the things and technologies used in the processes and communication between actors; rather, they are created together, in relation to each other. A teacher's reality is made up of the events that shape her experience and that make a difference. ANT examines how heterogeneous networks connect and manage to hold together, more or less temporarily, and how they enact economic, political and social phenomena or effects. Reality, and the actors enacted in it, is treated as an effect of the relations in the network. Actors are those who modify realities and make a difference in the world and are defined by what they do and how they perform (Latour, 1999, 2007). Latour (1993, p. 4) argues that 'this research does not deal with nature or knowledge, with things-in-themselves, but with the way all these things are tied to our collectives and to subjects'. As formulated within ANT,[2] reality is enacted in practice: 'ontologies are brought into being, sustained, or allowed to wither away in common, day to day, sociomaterial practices' (Mol, 2002, p. 6). Consequently, the performative dealings within ANT have to do with the socio-material processes taking place continuously, which draws attention to materiality and multiplicity and results in questions about 'multiple realities' and 'conflicting realities'. This means that different objects, including human subjects, will take different forms in different places and practices. Therefore, instead of asking 'What do teachers do when they make judgment about grades?' a more relevant question might be 'Where are grades?'

This would imply that entities of grading take different forms in different places and therefore it is relevant to trace the socio-material processes whereby, in this case, grading occurs as performances in webs of relations (Mulcahy, 2012). In this sense, grades and grading do not function as a representation of a fixed reality or as different perspectives of a fixed reality but as different realities enacted in different spaces with different functions and consequences. This is also a way of moving education out of the minds of individuals and placing it into networked spaces of political and social creation (Edwards & Clarke, 2002)—the notion that space is something performed rather than natural. Thus, space is made, or performed, in transactions.

Translations of associations

The associations or assemblages between human and non-human actors or elements shape networks that are contingent in relation to space and time. Therefore, time and space should not be viewed as a frozen background but rather as a variable of an assemblage (Edwards & Clarke, 2002). Space, as well as distance, is performed as an effect of heterogeneous socio-material relations (Fenwick & Edwards, 2012, p. xvii). In our empirical example, we examine how email technology changes the distance and space of a teacher's work and how this change of space affects her work in terms of grading and her role as a professional.

The factors that are collected in 'networks of associations' can be traced by translations. Translation refers to the negotiating processes that establish the relations of a network, where and when actors connect, and as they connect, change each other to coordinate (Callon, 1986; Latour, 1987, 1993). In this context, translation has the meaning of inducing two mediators into coexisting (Latour 2007), a concept that is useful when investigating how translation works. Latour differentiates between two different means to produce the social: *intermediaries* and *mediators*. These are moving entities that perform different functions in a network and that move things. Intermediaries transport meanings without translating or changing them in any way; the output is the same as the input, and they are fully defined by what causes it. Mediators 'transform, translate, distort, and modify the meaning or the elements they are supposed to carry' (Latour 2007, p. 39). A mediator, irrespective of how simple and uncomplicated its form appears, always exceeds its condition and produces complex meanings, which can lead to a multiplicity of (contradictory) directions (Latour, 1999, 2007). Actors are, as stated earlier, defined by how they perform in a network, and tracing the actors is about discovering in what way they behave, either as intermediaries or as mediators. This is where the symmetry between human and non-human actors becomes obvious. Humans can act as intermediaries in a network just as well as non-humans, and non-humans can often enact as mediators. The notions of translation, mediators and intermediaries help researchers trace how things come to be and how complex and messy processes and realities of education are enacted:

> [...] tracing exactly how entities are not just effects of their interaction with others, but are also always acting on others, subjugating others and making things possible. All are fragile, and all are powerful, held in balance with their interactions. None is inherently strong or weak, but only becomes strong by assembling other allies. (Fenwick & Edwards, 2012, p. xii)

The concept of translation denotes the shift from individual and psychological explanations of knowledge production towards interpretations of knowledge and learning as nested in social and cultural socio-material activities, forming networks that stretch over time and space, and connecting teachers with curricula, textbooks, students, grades, parental expectations or worries, computers, and other human and non-human actors. In this transaction, realities are enacted.

An analysis of a teacher's narrative of grades

Current research on the enacted curricula concerning grades and assessment indicates that teachers' conditions for action are related to the state's control system, national standards in curricula, and national tests (for examples from Swedish research, see Lundahl 2006; Selghed 2004; Tholin 2006). While governing structures are given a stronger position, teachers' room for acting at the same time is decreasing and vice versa. We argue that this perspective of mutual dependent balance or 'zero-sum game' might be too limited if one wants to explore the complex relations of impact the teacher is actually situated in. In today's society there are increasing demands on authorities in terms of transparency and accessibility, a development that, among other things, has been made possible by digital communications. In this respect, the school is no exception. The teacher is involved in a range of social systems, of which the school's governing system in certain cases might be assembled as one. In the empirical study, we trace the human and non-human actors in a delimited aspect of a teacher's work—that is, the task of grading students. By identifying different actors of concern, spaces of enactments of grading are revealed. The focus is directed towards the inner- and extra-institutional factors that form different, sometimes opposing, and sometimes overlapping assemblages that interact with this task, which is why we trace and examine how the relationships between, for example, teachers, grades, computers, students, parents and different places and spaces are organized. The empirical study is built on a narrative from an authentic interview with a named teacher in a Swedish newspaper in April, 2014[3]; however, we use a fictional name for the teacher and call her Susan.

The analysis is conducted in the following way. First, the actors are identified in the interview with Susan, actors that are more or less obviously enacting in networks. There are also obvious actors in our empirical example that we do not consider in this analysis, such as the newspaper article itself, the journalist, the purpose of the article, the readers of the newspaper and so on. The actors we focus on are the ones enacting Susan's reality when grading. Once actors are identified, we trace their various connections by asking questions about where the actors are placed, about how connections are made possible or made difficult, and about what relations are emphasized or obscured. How is the network translated? What actors enact as mediators and as translators? What actors enact as intermediaries, as unquestioned transporters of matters of fact? We then trace how the mediators change events and phenomena according to the interests and rationalities they represent in line with the notion of translation. In the case of Susan's story, we see that it is not only the content of emails between teachers and parents that have an impact but the email technology itself brings about an ontological change.

Susan is a teacher in one of Stockholm's most attractive upper secondary schools. The school is located in the inner city and only offers academic programmes. Susan was interviewed by one of Sweden's largest newspapers on the subject 'Teachers pressured to give high grades'. The article was written in response to a survey the newspaper has conducted together with one of Sweden's two teachers' organizations. The questionnaire that was sent to 1985 members of the teaching organization was answered by 1254 people, and 56% of the teachers who responded stated that parents' attempts to influence grading have increased over time. At schools where the parents of students are highly educated, 62% of the teachers indicated that pressures have increased, and in schools where parents have low to average education, 46% of the teachers stated that pressure from parents to give students a higher grade has increased.

Susan's story

Susan explains that students 'are not just pupils; they are also our customers. It becomes very clear'. Susan says that it is common that parents call the principal and say that 'this teacher has left incorrect grades; you must change it' or they accuse the teacher of miscon- duct. Other parents have urged the principal to replace teachers because of their grading. Susan was once reported to the School Inspectorate by a parent who was not satisfied with their child's grades. Susan emphasizes how important it is to get support from the principal in these situations. It is not all principals who endorse and support their teachers when they are exposed to parental pressure, according to Susan. At some schools, she has experienced principals who contribute to an implicit culture of satisfying the requests of students and parents; otherwise, there is a risk that students will choose to attend another school, in accordance with a market philosophy where students are viewed as customers. The school she works in at the moment is a popular school, with a high number of applications, which is why parental pressure does not have as much impact and the principal supports the teachers.

In the interview, Susan says that she spends a lot of time on long email conversations with parents discussing schoolwork, results and grades. Often, parents use their work email, showing that they have 'prestigious titles'. The discussions about grading, both with students in the classroom and with parents via email, are permeated with the assumption that the teacher is 'doing it wrong', referring to everything from teaching to assessing individual student achievement.

Susan really likes her job, but she often thinks about changing careers because of parental pressure, concealed threats, repeated illustrations of the low status of her profession, and because she spends too much time and energy on explaining herself to parents and students regarding assessment and grading.

A socio-material analysis of relations—where are grades?

Susan's story is about what her work consists of and how she handles her professional situ- ation. Her job as a teacher is placed in a network connected to the demands of a mar- ket-driven school system, where the means for the teachers to assess, evaluate and grade pupils are directly affected by how well-rated and popular the school is. Schools are depend- ent on how satisfied parents and students are with the school, as each school is financed by a voucher system. When looking at the actors involved in Susan's story, we find that both human and non-human actors and activities fill the workplace: parents and pupils (enacted as customers), supportive principals, not so supportive principals, grades, computers, email conversations, more or less concealed threats, parental engagement, and time.

One obvious material factor in Susan's story is the grades. Grades as such function as an intermediary, as a phenomenon that is taken for granted without being questioned. Grading functions as an inscription device; an entity materialized into a sign (Latour, 1999; Law, 2004, p. 160); and a reality translated into a letter. However, the specific grade that contains a distinct meaning related to a specific individual functions as a mediator that translates the materiality of a letter to a value, considered by an assemblage of a student, a teacher, parents, and a wider circle of friends, family, and educational institutions.

The assumption that teachers can grade pupils' real knowledge and capabilities is still challenged by some of the parents. Susan says 'Of course it is nicer and more straightforward when parents approach me directly'. But it is common that they call the principal instead for telling him/her that 'this teacher has left incorrect grades; you must change it'. Or they tell the principal to simply 'remove the teacher'. The question then arises whether grading and grades can be viewed as intermediaries any more, as they are contested. Nevertheless, it is not the possibility to grade or the grades themselves that are challenged by the parents at Susan's school; it is the individual teacher's ability to grade correctly that is in question. Is this particular teacher really capable of properly translating the correct reality into the correct letters? Thus, the phenomena of grading and grades as such remain unquestioned and therefore still function as intermediaries.

The principal at the school where Susan works tells the teachers on his staff that their task is to give correct grades without being influenced by outside factors, such as parental pressure. The principal acknowledges that this comes with a risk of further reports to the School Inspectorate from parents, but that this risk can be viewed as a sign that the teachers do their job as they should. Teachers' accountability is thus limited to their professional space, the school, as this is the space where supposedly correct grades are possible to find. It is in school that the teachers meet and talk to pupils; this is where lessons take place, where tests and assignments are made and delivered and where colleagues can be consulted.

What takes place in grading? Grades are expected to function as an intermediary, translating measurable knowledge into a grade. Susan's principal has expectations that the teachers will function as intermediaries without taking parental pressure into account, although in other schools the parents' and students' requests are expected to be met and satisfied and thus are included in the grading network as rather powerful actors. But although the principal supports Susan at her school, it does not mean that the parents are not actors in her networked reality when grading. Susan finds herself in a place where she needs the support and protection of the principal to do something she thinks is a part of the teaching profession. Accordingly, the parents are part of her network when grading, as is the principal.

The spaces where parents have influence have changed as an effect of the market-driven school system. Parents become responsible for making sure that their children get the best possible education, and the grades function as a confirmation that they have made the right choice. Parents thus become the markers of what a good school is, how it should work, and what it should result in. They naturally use email to communicate with teachers about their children, school assignments and grades. In Susan's story, using email in the communication between teachers, students and parents is not questioned as a phenomenon in itself but only in relation to the content of the communication. Nevertheless, it becomes obvious with a more symmetric view of the elements in the network that the email technology itself is a powerful actor, one that has a particularly tangible effect on Susan's professional and private lives. The email technology acts as a mediator, transporting and translating messages between teachers and parents, where parental dedication and worry turn into pressure and threats to the teacher. The computer places the parents almost literally in her living room in the evenings via its role as a mediator, translating the assemblage of computer, email technology, influential parents, and a prestigious school that is careful with its reputation—a gathering of the things that most significantly intrude into Susan's private life whether she decides to act upon them or not.

Susan stresses that after all, the dedication of parents is something positive. She says, 'Unfortunately, the students that need dedicated parents mostly do not have them'. The involvement and dedication of parents is something both needed and problematic for Susan. In this statement, it appears that when the parental involvement moves into the teacher's space it becomes a problem; it turns into something pressing and threatening for the teacher. When it is directed towards the student's space, dedication means something else; it means help with homework, encouragement, and so on. In other words, involvement is something desirable.

Susan's social sphere is affected and changed by email technology, and the boundary between teacher Susan and private Susan becomes vaguer. The borders between workplace and home and between working and free time are blurred. Susan spends lots of time and energy on page-long email conversations with parents who question her judgement when grading. The email not only provides a new way of communicating, but it profoundly changes her spatial and temporal working conditions. The conversation has been removed from the actual physical school, and it most certainly has spread from Susan's working hours into her free time and from her work place into her home. But most importantly, this 'new' kind of conversation also takes place in terms of new roles. Susan tells of parents using their work emails, showing their 'distinguished titles'. Susan says: 'It becomes obvious that you, as a teacher, don't have the highest status in their eyes. The whole school situation is permeated by pupils and parents assuming that teachers are doing everything wrong when it comes to planning, teaching, and assessment'. Conversing with the teacher from the workplace email enables the parent not only to play the role of the concerned parent, but they also display the power that their 'distinguished title' provides. In Susan's case, it is obvious that she notices and is affected by the performativity of the parents' titles. Email has expanded the spaces of grading to include the principal's office, the homes and workplaces of the parents, and the homes of the teachers. This displacement of space changes the position of the teacher and the teacher's availability, accountability and ability to act within the new spaces. However, the most problematic aspect of the expanded time and space seems to be the change in whom she becomes and who the parents become in their communication; that is, limitations and extensions respectively in their roles and status. Questions also arise about what it might mean to teachers when their availability changes. What can teachers be held accountable for? And where?

What Susan is telling us in this interview is that a new strong social force has been brought to the fore by the translation between the internet with its email system and the school that makes it easy for parents to email their children's teachers and put the teachers in a situation where they are expected to respond to every email and to explain themselves to the parents. The network that has long since been established in the classroom through the conversations between the teacher and his/her students before, during and after class has now been expanded to include parents' and teachers' work and home environments by the provision of access to email. An important basis for this expansion is the marketization of the Swedish school system, implemented by a voucher system where every student represents a certain sum of money for the school. Thus, the voucher system also affects the network of teaching and grading and must be viewed as a vital part in that network. Instead of being a professional concern for the teacher, grades become an ambiguous phenomena depending on who and what is included in the process and also where this process takes place.

What can be learned from Susan's story is that in order to function in their professional roles as teachers, teachers need clear and strong support from the local and national school system to maintain sufficient autonomy in their professional work. As illustrated by Susan's story, teachers are nested in complicated material and non-material assemblages of social relations that risk affecting their professional work by placing them in situations where time and space make them vulnerable due to the confusion of public and private spaces.

A 'performance-based' reality

In this article, we have taken our starting point in transactional realism. Dewey's piecemeal realism, expressed through his carefully elaborated concept of experience, is characterized by the significance of time and space; that is, thinking depends on our coordinates in space-time (Semetsky, 2006). This temporality and contingency of space have, or so we argue, an affinity with an the ANT understanding of 'the social' as exceeding time and space in the performance of the social. 'A book or a letter may institute a more intimate association between human beings separated thousands of miles from each other than exists between dwellers under the same roof' (Dewey, 1916/2008, p. 7). Thus, temporality and potentiality constitute an intersection between transactional realism and ANT. Another intersection point between transactional realism and ANT is constituted by the recognition of the influence of non-human factors. In Dewey's words, material phenomena 'express the ways in which things act upon another and upon us; the ways in which, when objects act together, they reinforce and interfere' (Dewey, 1934/1980, pp. 100–101). Latour (2007, p. 116, *italics in original*) goes a step further and shifts the attention from a world of matters of fact to 'the *worlds* of matters of concern', making room for inquiries of the agency of all sort of objects.

Latour is not interested in dissolving the boundaries between human and non-human objects but in going beyond these limits by asking the question: Does this agent make a difference in the course of some other agent's action? In ANT, then, '*any thing* that does modify a state of affairs by making a difference is an actor' (Latour, 2007, p. 71). Humans and objects are distinct, but 'difference is not a divide'; instead, they are 'woven into the *same* stories' (p. 76 fn.) The affinity between transactional realism and ANT that we have drawn attention to does not mean that they are the same. What we argue is that ANT can contribute to the theory of transactional realism by emphasizing the performativity of matter when trying to grasp what constitutes *an* experience. We perceive similarities between the unforeseen and becoming in an experience in the way Dewey defines the concept and the form of momentary association that defines the social within ANT. Here, ANT can contribute to and develop the understanding of what constitutes an experience in-between different forms of objects—both material and non-material. What the theory of transaction contributes to ANT is a philosophical idea of how the social is formed in terms of a genuine environment of 'the things with which a man *varies*' (Dewey, 1916/2008, p. 15). Further, transactional realism contributes to ANT's understanding of 'the political' as performativity with the insight that change and renewal constitute conditions with political relevance without being able to decide the space of 'the public' or judge the consequences of 'the political' beforehand.

Neither ANT nor transactional realism understands 'the public' as a 'thing' with demarcated borders. The public is a gathering of people concerned with the consequences of a communicative transaction, of a shared problem. The public is always in the making, always changing in terms of size and affairs. When we ask 'Where are grades?', we are looking at what assemblages become visible when gathering a more heterogeneous set of actors into the analysis of what constitutes the social (Law, 2004, Mol, 2002). The aim is not in the first place to find solutions to Susan's problem but rather to find out how it became a problem for her in the first place. Bringing material aspects into the consideration of Susan's situation helps us see that it is the technology itself that changes the spaces and moves grading into several spaces where Susan does not have professional authority. In Susan's case, the public—in the form of parents, students and the school system—is invading her private life. These actions are political but not as a whole. They are political in the way they are traced to new associations and designing new assemblages. ANT asks us to think in terms of nodes that have as many dimensions as they have connections, explaining the effects of the collected networks that make up our socio-material world. When power is understood as effect rather than causes (Clarke, 2002), power relations become visible in new spaces. In Susan's case, the parental power over school and teachers' work is problematic, but it becomes most crucial for Susan when this power spreads into spaces where she becomes diminished by it, giving her less room for action in the network of grading that is her professional responsibility. The email technology is not a silent or neutral artefact in this network, which stands outside of the social and the public. It is a mediating part of it, and it takes a significant part in changing Susan's professional role and sphere.

By drawing attention to the role of technology, we also become aware of how the boundaries between the private and the public have been displaced. According to Latour (2011, p. 11), what Dewey calls 'the public' has a 'striking similarity' to the so-called precautionary principle. For Latour (2011, p. 12), this principle means a call for 'experimentation, invention, exploration, and of course risk taking' in the decision-making of our daily lives. While Dewey relies on naturalism (Sleeper, 1986/2001), Latour argues for multinaturalism. In Latour's interpretation, nature is how we define the world we have in common, 'the obvious existence we share, the sphere to which we all pertain equally' (2011, p. 8). There are many competing natures and worlds, and this is what gives nature a political dimension. When material factors, such as technology, are left out of what constitutes the public and are accordingly treated as non-political and natural matters of course, it becomes harder to question their place and agency. Bringing a socio-materialist logic into a pragmatic exploration of what matters for teachers and in what ways teachers matter, provides a more complex understanding of how the social is enacted, what becomes of concern, and where the social takes place. Technologies do not only change the conditions for our lives, but also who we become in the world. What the common world is and what role technology should play in it is a question for the public to engage in, and to experiment on with care and caution.

Notes

1. Regarding the term 'post-postmodernism', see Hickman, 2007.
2. It is important to note that ANT cannot be treated as one unified and concordant theory but rather as a disparate set of tools, sensibilities, and methods of analysis (Fenwick & Edwards, 2010; Law, 2007). However, we will refer to this disparity as ANT.
3. Svenska Dagbladet 25 April 2014.

Disclosure statement

No potential conflict of interest was reported by the authors.

References

Beck, U., & Grande, E. (2007). *Cosmopolitan Europe*. Cambridge: Polity Press.

Bennett, J. (2010). *Vibrant matter: A political ecology of things*. Durham, NC: Duke University Press.

Bernstein, R. J. (2010). *The pragmatic turn*. Cambridge: Polity.

Bhaskar, R. (1997). *A realist theory of science*. London: Verso.

Biesta, G. (2014). Pragmatising the curriculum: Bringing knowledge back into the curriculum conversation, but via pragmatism. *The Curriculum Journal, 25*, 29–49.

Callon, M. (1986). Some elements of a sociology of translation: Domestication of the scallops and the fishermen of St Brieuc Bay. In J. Law (Ed.), *Power, action, belief: A new sociology of knowledge* (pp. 196–233). London: Routledge.

Clarke, J. (2002). A new kind of symmetry. Actor-network theories and the new literacy studies. *Studies in the Education of Adults, 34*, 107–122.

Davidson, D. (1991/2001). Three varieties of knowledge. In D. Davidson (Ed.), *Subjective, intersubjective, objective* (pp. 205–220). Oxford: Clarendon Press.

Dewey, J. (1916/2008). Democracy and education. In J. A. Boydston (Ed.), *John Dewey. The middle works, 1899–1924, volume 9: 1916* (pp. 3–370). Carbondale: Southern Illinois University Press.

Dewey, J. (1917/1985). The need for a recovery of philosophy. In J. A. Boydston (Ed.), *John Dewey. The middle works, 1899–1924, volume 10: 1916–1917* (pp. 3–48). Carbondale: Southern Illinois University Press.

Dewey, J. (1927/1991). *The public and its problems*. Athens, OH: Swallow Press.

Dewey, J. (1934/1980). *Art as experience*. New York: Perigee.

Edwards, R., & Clarke, J. (2002). Flexible learning, spatiality and identity. *Studies in Continuing Education, 24*, 153–165.

Fenwick, T., & Edwards, R. (2010). *Actor-network – Theory in education*. London: Routledge.

Fenwick, T., & Edwards, R. (2012). Introduction. In T. Fenwick & R. Edwards (Eds.), *Researching education through actor-network theory* (pp. ix–xxiii). Malden, MA: Wiley-Blackwell.

TEACHERS MATTER – BUT HOW?

Fenwick, T., Edwards, R., & Sawchuk, P. (2011). *Emerging approaches to educational research: Tracing the sociomaterial*. Oxon: Routledge.

Ferraris, M. (2014). *Manifest för en ny realism* [Manifesto for a new realism]. Göteborg: Daidalos.

Garrison, J. (1994). Realism, Deweyan pragmatism, and educational research. *Educational Researcher, 23*, 5–14.

Garrison, J. (1999). John Dewey, Jacques Derrida, and the metaphysics of presence. *Transactions of Charles S. Peirce Society, XXXV*, 346–372).

Hickman, L. A. (2007). *Pragmatism as post-postmodernism: Lessons from John Dewey*. New York, NY: Fordham University Press.

Johansson, L. (2015). *Tillblivelsens pedagogik: Om att utmana det förgivettagna* [A pedagogy of becoming: Challenging the obvious] (Doctoral dissertation), Lund University, Lund.

Latour, B. (1987). *Science in action: How to follow scientists and engineers through society*. Cambridge, MA: Harvard University Press.

Latour, B. (1993). *We have never been modern*. Cambridge, MA: Harvard University Press.

Latour, B. (1999). *Pandora's hope: Essays on the reality of science studies*. Cambridge, MA: Harvard University Press.

Latour, B. (2007). *Reassembling the social: An introduction to action-network-theory*. Oxford: Oxford University Press.

Latour, B. (2011). From multiculturalism to multinaturalism: What rules of method for the new socio-scientific experiments? *Nature and Culture, 6*(1), 1–17.

Law, J. (2003). *Traduction/trahison: Notes on ANT*. Centre for Science Studies, Lancaster University. Retrieved from http://www.comp.lancs.ac.uk/sociology/papers/Law-Traduction-Trahison.pdf

Law, J. (2004). *After method: Mess in social science research*. New York, NY: Routledge.

Law, J. (2007). Making a mess with method. In W. Outhwaite & S. P. Turner (Eds.), *The SAGE handbook of social science methodology* (pp. 595–606). London: Sage.

Lundahl, C. (2006). *Viljan att veta vad andra vet. Kunskapsbedömning i tidigmoder, modern och senmodern skola* [To know what others know: Assessment in education in premodern, modern and late-modern times] (Doctoral dissertation), Arbetslivsinstitutet, Stockholm.

Mol, A. (2002). *The body multiple: Ontology in medical practice*. Durham, NC: Duke University Press.

Moore, R., & Young, M. (2010). Reconceptualizing knowledge and the curriculum in the sociology of education. In K. Maton & R. More (Eds.), *Social realism, knowledge and the sociology of education* (pp. 14–34). London: Continuum.

Mulcahy, D. (2012). Assembling the 'accomplished' teacher: The performativity and politics of professional teaching standards. In T. Fenwick & R. Edwards (Eds.), *Researching education through actor-network theory* (pp. 78–96). Malden, MA: Wiley-Blackwell.

Rorty, R. (Ed.). (1992). *The linguistic turn: Essays in philosophical method*. Chicago: The University of Chicago Press.

Rosiek, J. (2013). Pragmatism and post-qualitative futures. *International Journal of Qualitative Studies in Education, 26*, 692–705.

Selghed, B. (2004). *Ännu icke godkänt. Lärares sätt att erfara betygssystemet och dess tillämpning i yrkesutövningen* [Not yet approved. Teachers' ways of experiencing the grading system and its application in professional practice] (Doctoral dissertation), Malmö Studies in Educational Sciences No. 15, Malmö.

Semetsky, I. (2006). *Deleuze, education and becoming*. Rotterdam: Sense.

Sleeper, R. W. (1986/2001). *The necessity of pragmatism: John Dewey's conception of philosophy*. Urbana: University of Illinois Press.

Tholin, J. (2006). *Att kunna klara sig i ökänd natur. En studie av betyg och betygskriterier – historiska betingelser och implementering av ett nytt system* [Being able to cope in a notorious nature. A study of grades and grading criteria – Historical conditions and the implementation of a new system] (Doctoral dissertation), Högskolan i Borås, Borås.

Wahlström, N. (2010). Learning to communicate or communicating to learn? A conceptual discussion on communication, meaning and knowledge. *Journal of Curriculum Studies, 42*, 431–449.

Westbrook, R. B. (1991). *John Dewey and American democracy*. Ithaca, NY: Cornell University Press.

Westbrook, R. B. (2005). *Democratic hope: Pragmatism and the politics of truth*. Ithaca, NY: Cornell University Press.

Wheelahan, L. (2010). *Why knowledge matters in curriculum: A social realist argument*. London: Routledge.

Young, M. F. D. (2008). *Bringing knowledge back in: From social constructivism to social realism in the sociology of education*. London: Routledge.

Index

Note: Italic page numbers refer to figures. Page numbers followed by "n" refer to endnotes.

accountability: educational 24, 55–7, 59, 70, *77*; organizational 90; policies 8, 88; public education 56; *see also* technical accountability, curriculum policy in
actor–network theory (ANT) 5, 97, 99, 100, 106, 107
agency 2; chordal triad of 52n1; definition of 52n1; ecological view of 40; projective dimension of 51; theory of 40; *see also* teacher agency and talk
Alexander, R. 25, 26
altruistic ethic 83, 84
American schools, accountability and control 5; centralization/decentralization 79; economic competitiveness 75; educational accountability theory *77*; education system 80; effective and ineffective 86; faculty influence *87*; financial subsidization of 85; Indicators of Education Systems project 79; international differences *81*; occupation of teaching 85; Organisation for Economic Co-operation and Development 79, 80; organizational accountability 90; performance 89, *89*; power and control 77, 80; principals and teachers, relative influence *81, 82*; Programme for International Student Assessment 79; reform movement 76; Schools and Staffing Survey 78–81, 85–8; teacher accountability perspective 76, 77, 88; Teacher Follow-up Survey 78–9; teachers and teaching quality 75; teachers' responsibility 83–6; top-down reforms 89, 90; traditional public school approach 76
Andrews, Kay 33
ANT *see* actor–network theory
arts-based research 9

balanced approach 5, 90
Ball, S. J. 57, 60

'bearing witness' to teaching and teachers 3–4; accountability policies 8; aesthetic capacities 12; arts-based research 9; concept of 20n1; connoisseurship 9; context for study 8; dimensions of witnessing 18; distance and nearness 17–19; educational policy and research 19–20; ethical proximity 12–17; ethics, notion of 11; field notes 10–11, 13; good teaching 8; idea 9; importance 19–20; intellectual dimension 12; Karolina's case 10–11; knowledge production 12; modes of research 8–9; orientation 9–11; phenomenology 8–9; portraiture 9; readiness 16–17; Robertson's work 21n7; 'self-witness' 18; wisdom and love 19; witness, concept of 7
Benhabib, S. 24, 26–8
Bernstein, R. J. 98
Biesta, Gert 4
Braun, A. 60
Braun, V. 62
Brennan, M. 64
Buchmann, M. 20n2

capability approach: cosmopolitanism and 27–32; human diversity and 29
Cherryholmes, C. H. 2
Clarke, V. 62
'collective experiment' 99
Collins, Gregory 5
conflicting realities 100
connoisseurship 9
Cook, I. 67
cosmopolitanism: and capabilities 27–32; concerns of 34; in political philosophy 28
critical realism 97; *see also* realism
Curriculum for Excellence 39, 42, 44, 45, 47–8
curriculum, temporal understanding of 1–2

datafication 56, 57, 69
data management system 65–6
'de-humanisation' 5

INDEX

Deleuze, Gilles 99
'deliverology', features of 60
democratic iteration 4; in classroom 33; concept 26; features 32; and pedagogic relations 25–7, 31
democratic legitimacy 26
detachment 17–18
Dewey, J. 5, 9, 97–9; experience concept 97–8; and Latour, B. 99; logic of theory 98; nature, concept of 97; piecemeal realism 98, 106; pragmatism 99; *Public and Its Problems, The* 99; transactional realism 97
disciplinary-based curriculum 64
distance, in witnessing 17–19
diverse obligations 27–32
Dustin, C. A. 15

education: biographical experiences 4, 41–3, 45–6; career outside of 47–9; as difficult process 46; environment 3; policy discourse of learning 46–7; vocabulary 49, 50
educational accountability 24, 55–7, 59, 70, *77*
educational criticism 9
educational policy-making, technical–rational discourse of 5
Eisner, Elliot 9
elementary and secondary schooling 75, 86
email technology 105
Emirbayer, M. 2, 40, 52n1
England, educational problems in 56
English Baccalaurate (E-Bac) 63, 66, 71n4
English secondary schools 4; 'deliverology', features of 60; education system 65; 'fixing' teachers and students 67–9; GCSE examination performance in 63
Epstein, M. 12
equalities 25–32; injustice and 26, 28, 32–4; pedagogic relationships and 32–4; *see also* inequalities
equity: concept 25; critical engagement with 32; features 32; forms 27–32; in schooling 66
ethical proximity, and witnessing 12–17
ethical responsibility 60–1

Fataar, A. 64
Ferraris , M. 97
Finnish education system 25
'fixing' curriculum knowledge 63–7

Garrison, J. 25
General Certificate of Secondary Education (GCSE) 61, 63–5
global inequalities, *see* equalities
global injustice 4; feature of 29; and inequality 26, 28, 29, 34; pedagogic relationships with 32
Guattari, Félix 99

Hansen, David 1, 3–4, 28, 31
heterogeneous networks 99, 100

horizontal inequalities 29–31
Hoskins, K. 60
humanness, notion of 59

Ignatieff, M. 27
implicit curriculum 2
Indicators of Education Systems (INES) project 79
inequalities 4; different facets of 29–30, 32; features of 29, 32; and global injustice 26, 28, 29, 34; horizontal 29–31; procedural 29–30, 32; vertical 29–30, 32
INES project *see* Indicators of Education Systems project
Ingersoll, Richard 5
injustice 34; and global inequalities 26, 28, 32–4; pedagogy and 32–4
intermediaries 101, 102, 104
international economic environment 56
International Survey of the Locus of Decision-Making in Educational Systems, The 79, 91n1

Key Stage 4 (KS4) 61, 65
knowledge-based economy 55
knowledge-based occupations 90
knowledge production 12
KS4 *see* Key Stage 4

language of learning 41
Latour, B. 99, 100, 106, 107
levels of progress (LPs) 65
Levinas, E. 58, 60–1
Lingard, B. 57, 58
linguistic pragmatism 98
Lortie, D. 83
'lower ability' students 69

Maguire, M. 60
Marchand, André 15
mediators 101
Miller, Jerome 16
Mische, A. 2, 40, 52n1
MLS Project *see* Moral Life of Schools Project
Moore, A. 25
Moral Life of Schools (MLS) Project 20n1
multiple realities 100

National Center for Educational Statistics (NCES) 78
National Curriculum Attainment Levels 65
national/federal education authority 79
NCES *see* National Center for Educational Statistics
nearness, in witnessing 17–19
neo-liberalism 57
networks of associations 101
'new language of learning' 41
new materialism 96, 97
No Child Left Behind Act (NCLB) 5, 77, 80
null curriculum 2

INDEX

OECD *see* Organisation for Economic Co-operation and Development
official curriculum 2
Omaar, L. 34
ontological insecurity 57
Organisation for Economic Co-operation and Development (OECD) 1, 79, 80, 85

'partnership schools' 90
pedagogy 4, 34; complexity 32, 34; definition 26; democratic iterations with 31; and inequalities 32–4; and injustices 32–4; relationships 25–7; teachers engaged 30; in transnational classroom 32–4; work by teachers 29
performance-based reality 106–7
performative education system 57
performative improvement 56
performativity carries, concept of 57
piecemeal realism 98, 106
PISA *see* Programme for International Student Assessment
policy documents 1
portraiture 8, 9, 12
'post-postmodern' approach 96
precautionary principle 107
Priestley, Mark 4
procedural inequalities 29–30, 32
professional identities, of teachers 2
Programme for International Student Assessment (PISA) 25, 29, 32, 79
'Progress Over Time' 65
Public and Its Problems, The (Dewey) 99
public education accountability 56
public service ethic 83

Ranson, S. 55
'raw material' of education 58
realism 5–6; conflicting 100; critical 97; Deleuze, Gilles 99; grading students 97; Guattari, Félix 99; human and non-human actors 99, 103; multiple 100; narrative of grades 102–3; overview 96–7; performance-based 106–7; piecemeal 98; reflexive 96; social 97; socio-material analysis of relations 103–6; Susan's case study 103–6; transactional 97, 107; translations of associations 101–2; *see also* Dewey, J.
reflexive realism 96
regulatory curriculum system 70
Rizvi , F. 58
Robinson, Sarah 4
Rorty, R. 98
Rousseau, Jean-Jacques 15

Sahlberg, P. 25
Schools and Staffing Survey (SASS) 78–81, 85–8
schools' management information system (SIMS) 65, 66
'self-witness' 18

Sen, A. 29
Shulman, L. S. 38
SIMS *see* schools' management information system
social constructivist approach 99
social engineering research 9
social realism 97
socio-material analysis of relations 103–6
socio-material processes 100, 101
standardized programme 59
standardized test scores 77
Starkey, H. 28
Stewart, F. 29
Stobart, G. 55
subjectivity: and education 59; ethical responsibility 60–1; technical accountability 59–60
Sundström-Sjödin, Elin 5–6
sustained silent reading (SSR) 13

teacher agency and talk 4, 39; achievement 4; age and generation 43–4; biographical experiences 41–3, 45–6; career outside of education 47–9; curriculum and 1–2; *Curriculum for Excellence* 39, 42, 44, 45, 47–8; definition 3; discourses 40–1; ecological approach 39–41; personal and professional 44–5; policy discourses 46–7; as reconstructions 2; shaping an educational outlook 49–51; talk about education 41–3, 45–6; teacher knowledge 38–9; theory of agency 40; vocabularies 40, 51–2
'teacher-deficit' assumption 77
Teacher Follow-up Survey (TFS) 78–9
teacher knowledge 4; propositional/theoretical knowledge 39; Shulman's distinction of 38; 'stock of knowledge' 39
teacher policy: documents 1; OECD report 1
Teachers Matter: Attracting, Developing and Retaining Effective Teachers (2005) 1
teaching: as curriculum process 2; as moral activity 3
technical accountability, curriculum policy in 4–5, 58; characteristics 56; core and content knowledge 63–4; data management system 65–6; de-professionalization experience 68; educational problems 56; English Baccalaurate 63; evaluation 55; 'fix', analytical concept of 62–3; General Certificate of Secondary Education 61, 63–5; interpretation 58; levels of progress 65; pedagogy and relationships 58; performative improvement 56; performativity carries 57; power 58–9; subjectivity 59–61; *see also* English secondary schools
technical evidence base 66
technical–rational accounting system 57, 63, 70
'test-based metrics' 57
TFS *see* Teacher Follow-up Survey

113

INDEX

Thompson, G. 67
Thoreau, Henry David 15
Todd, S. 58
Tokuda, M. 33
transactional realism 5, 97, 106, 107
translations of associations 101–2
transnational classroom, pedagogy in 32–4
truth telling 9

Unterhalter, Elaine 4

'value-added' model 76
vertical inequalities 29–30, 32
vocabularies 38, 40, 51–2

Wahlström, Ninni 5–6
Westbrook, R. B. 98
Winter, Christine 4–5
witnessing: distance and nearness
    17–19; ethical proximity and 12–17;
    see also 'bearing witness' to teaching
    and teachers

Yates, L. 64
Young, M. 25, 26

'zero-sum game' 102
Ziegler, J. E. 15
Zipin, L. 64